ASSASSINATION IN VIENNA

ASSASSINATION IN VIENNA

Walter B. Maass

CHARLES SCRIBNER'S SONS | NEW YORK

Printed in the United States of America
Library of Congress Catalog Card Number 71-162772
SBN 684-12587-0

TO META

*for her help and encouragement
in writing this book*

Contents

Illustrations

PICTURE CREDITS

Austrian Institute of Contemporary History, 118 (both). Austrian
National Library, 113, 114, 115, 116 (both), 117, 119, 121 (both,
122 (both), 123, 124. Palphot Agency, Jerusalem, 125. United Press
International, 120.

Maps

Maps by Robert Sugar

ASSASSINATION IN VIENNA

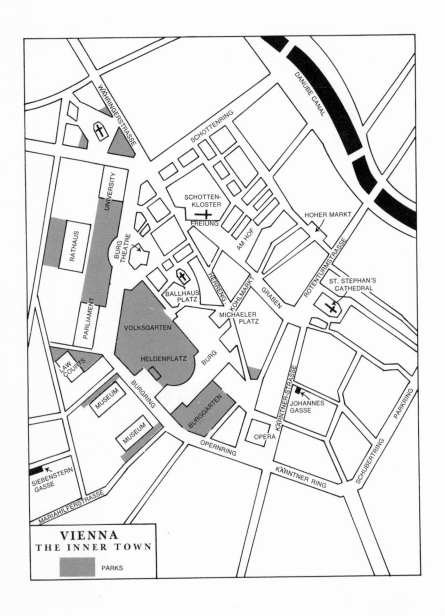

VIENNA
THE INNER TOWN

PARKS

Preface

THIS BOOK DEALS WITH an episode of Austrian history: the
conspiracy against the government of Engelbert Dollfuss, which led to his murder on July 25, 1934. That
event was one of the steppingstones to the destruction of the
Austrian Republic. The final action was the collapse of the
Austrian government on March 11, 1938, followed by the
invasion of German troops. By this operation Austria was
temporarily wiped off the map. In fact, it became a country
without a name, a mere province of the Third Reich, only to
be restored when Hitler's imperium fell to pieces. The period
from 1918 to 1938 is now referred to as the era of the First
Austrian Republic. The present Austrian state, which was
born during the last days of World War II, and which regained its full sovereignty on May 15, 1955, is called the
Second Republic.

1

The intention of the author is to describe a strange and fateful interlude which led to Dollfuss's assassination. For the understanding of the reader it is necessary to explain the situation in which Dollfuss and his government had found themselves in 1934. The events after July 1934 are briefly described in the epilogue.

The sources on which this book relies are mainly Austrian and German documents and memoirs, and two biographical works on Dollfuss by British authors J. D. Gregory and G. Brook-Shepherd, both of which are informative but rather partial. Several persons who were involved in the July events have written books containing valuable material: Kurt von Schuschnigg, Ernst Ruediger von Starhemberg, Friedrich Funder, Franz Winkler, Anton Rintelen, Franz von Papen. All these men had some personal part in the tragedy.

Highly important for the understanding of the Nazi revolt in Austria is the official report which the Austrian government published shortly after the event. This publication on the preliminaries and facts of the uprising contains much vital information, though certain facets regarding the part played by Minister Emil Fey were tampered with.

Three reports from the Nazi side are also of great importance. G. O. Waechter and R. Weydenhammer, both leaders of the putsch, wrote descriptions of the uprising, but only after the Anschluss in 1938. Those papers are very subjective, especially the one by Waechter, who was defending himself against the accusation of having mismanaged the whole affair and having acted against the will of Hitler.

In 1964, a number of SS documents were found in Czechoslovakia. Among them was a "Report of the Historical Commission of the Reichsfuehrer SS regarding the uprising of the Austrian National Socialists in July 1934." This study, undertaken in 1938, is based on the two earlier ones by Waechter and Weydenhammer and contains a great deal of material. It seems that the report should have formed the basis of an accusation and trial against the former Austrian Chancellor Schuschnigg, who at that time was a prisoner of the Nazis. However, the Nazi authorities seem to have judged the material insufficient. Actually, no trial against Schuschnigg ever took place, and the papers rested peacefully in some file for twenty-five years.

Thus we have considerable information from both sides about what happened in Vienna on Wednesday, July 25, 1934. In spite of that wealth of sources, a number of facts have never been fully explained and will perhaps forever remain mysterious. Did Hitler order the assassination of Dollfuss? Why did the Austrian Chancellor stay at the Ballhausplatz, though he knew that an attack against the seat of government was in progress? Was Dollfuss's death planned in advance or was it due to the hasty action of a trigger-happy rebel? Why were the authorities so slow in reacting when the plot was betrayed? What was the true part of Major Fey in all these strange events? Was the Austrian government justified in capturing and prosecuting the rebels after a safe-conduct had been granted to them?

In the following pages the author has told the full story which reads in part like a spy thriller and has all the trappings of a musical-comedy plot. I have adhered strictly to the facts. Nothing has been invented; and in those instances where the facts are doubtful, I have tried to relate all possible conclusions.

I am a native of Vienna and was a student at the University there when the events described in this book occurred. On the day of the revolt I happened to be in Bad Ischl, an ancient spa in Upper Austria. I heard the news while having cake and coffee at Zauner, the famous pastry shop of that resort place.

A fellow student, serving in the Heimwehr, told me that an attack had been made on the Vienna Chancellery. For the rest of the day my girl and I sat glued to the radio, but the news was very confusing. Only late in the evening did we hear that Dollfuss was dead.

My main memory of those days is an atmosphere of doom and uncertainty. On the next morning a great number of hotel guests and tourists convened on the local esplanade and stood in stony silence while the orchestra played the "Marche Funèbre" by Chopin. Normally the orchestra entertained the public with operetta tunes. Among the listeners I remember three famous composers: Franz Lehar, Emmerich Kalman, and Oscar Straus; Bad Ischl was the meeting place of the theater crowd.

On the walls of some European churches and cloisters a strange allegory is depicted. It shows Death, either a skeleton or a corpse in its shroud, leading a variety of people to a dance. Art historians believe that those frescoes date from the era of great disasters, long wars, or perhaps epidemics. For Austria, the death of Dollfuss started such a *danse macabre.* Of the many thousands who listened to the funeral marches, not only in Bad Ischl but all over the country, a great number would die by violence during the following decade. The death of the little Chancellor in Vienna was the first sinister signal of future horrors. It announced the coming of a new order, the carrier of madness and destruction. That power was to rage over the land until it was ground to dust in ravaged, flaming cities. On July 25, 1934, the dance of death was just beginning, and those who listened to the music of the funeral march merely felt a slight shudder of things to come.

1

The Warning

IT WAS ONE OF THOSE very hot summer days which most Viennese prefer to spend out of town. Many people of prominence had already left for vacation. The President of the Republic, Wilhelm Miklas, had gone to Velden in Carinthia. The Vice Chancellor, Prince Ernst Ruediger von Starhemberg, and his girl friend were resting at the Lido near Venice. The Chancellor himself, Dr. Engelbert Dollfuss, was still in Vienna but planned to join his wife and children, who were the private guests of his friend and protector Benito Mussolini, at Riccione on the Adriatic. In fact, he had recently taken swimming lessons, for his host was an expert swimmer and he, Dollfuss, did not wish to cut a poor figure on the beach. The Austrian ambassador in Rome had also gone on vacation, but in the opposite direction. Dr. Anton Rintelen, undaunted by the heat, was stationed at the Hotel Imperial in

Vienna. It did not bother him that the city was half empty, smoldering indolently in the sun, with the opera and almost all the theaters closed.

The middle-aged man, who walked nervously down the Lerchenfelderstrasse, was clearly not on vacation. Like the typical Austrian civil servant he carried a briefcase, and he kept furtively looking over his shoulder as if he feared to be pursued. When he finally reached his destination, the Café Weghuber, he marched right into the telephone booth without even bothering to order coffee. The number he called was the one of the central office of the Fatherland Front—Austria's only political organization. He asked for the federation's chief, Mr. Stepan, but was told that the boss was presently not at his desk. "Well, tell him to come immediately to the Café Weghuber at the Museumstrasse. I have some most important information for him. I cannot give you my name, but tell him that it is a vital matter!" He hung up and wiped his brow. Then he sat down and ordered coffee and rolls. He picked up a newspaper and read that a man had been executed for throwing a bomb and killing a policeman. It was not quite clear whether the delinquent had been a socialist or a Nazi. He put the newspaper away, visibly perturbed. Everything was very quiet. The few guests were breakfasting peacefully or reading their papers. It was now 8:15 A.M.

Two hours passed and nothing happened. Another gentleman with a briefcase walked in, was profusely greeted by the headwaiter, sat down and ordered coffee. The first man watched him intently, suddenly got up and stepped to the newcomer's table. "Excuse me," he said, in a voice hoarse with emotion. "I believe I have seen you here before. Are you not a member of the Heimwehr?"[1] The gentleman rose politely and introduced himself. He said his name was Karl

---

1. Heimwehr means "Home Guard." It was a paramilitary organization.

Mahrer, and indeed he was an official of the Heimwehr organization, a district collector of membership dues. He invited
the other man to sit down at his table, watching him with a
mixture of curiosity and compassion. It was quite obvious that
the poor fellow was in some kind of distress. His hands trem-
bled and he was sweating profusely. Speaking almost in a
whisper, he kept nervously glancing around as if he expected
to be attacked at any moment. Finally he pulled himself together and showed Mahrer his credentials, a police card with
authentic rubber stamps and a photo of the bearer, made out
to Johann Dobler, Inspector of Police of the sixteenth pre-
cinct. Karl Mahrer was left in no doubt that he was speaking
to a plainclothesman of the city's police force.

But the tale the nervous man now poured out to his astonished listener sounded fantastic. Dobler claimed that an
armed revolt against the government of Chancellor Dollfuss
was afoot. He, Johann Dobler, was himself a member of the
illegal Nazi Party and the conspiracy. But he had changed his
mind. He was now ready to denounce the whole venture and
thereby save Austria from being taken over by the Nazis.

Mahrer listened in stupefaction. If all this were true, why
would Dobler approach him, a mere district collector, a minor
official? Why not go straight to the police? Why did the inspector not simply inform his superior officer?

He received a shocking reply. Several high police officers
were themselves involved in the plot. In fact, the police force
was riddled with Nazis from top to bottom. Therefore, said
Dobler, he feared that his report would fall into the wrong
hands. Only ten days ago another policeman by the name of
Zimmer had been murdered because the Nazis suspected him
of defection. Dobler was afraid to share his fate if he worked
through the usual channels at the police department. For that
reason he had phoned the Fatherland Front office two hours
ago and asked its chief to come immediately to the Café

Weghuber. But nobody had arrived yet and time was running short. The armed revolt would start at 12:15 P.M.; it was now 10 A.M. and the government was still unaware of the danger. Therefore he had decided to confide in Mahrer, whom he vaguely remembered as a member of the patriotic Heimwehr organization.

Perhaps Mahrer was still only half-convinced, but now Dobler became more specific. He admitted being a Nazi but one who for some time had been most uncomfortable about the object and methods of the party. He had no desire to turn traitor to his own country and was not willing to take part in an armed uprising. However, such a revolt would now take place within hours if the government remained ignorant of the plot and, consequently, inactive. At 12:15 P.M. a Nazi striking force of about 150 men would assemble in a gymnasium at the Siebensterngasse. He, Dobler, had received written orders to join it. The insurgents, disguised as regular soldiers, would be driven in trucks to the chancellery at the Ballhausplatz, while the Cabinet was in session. They would occupy the building and arrest the whole government. Then, Anton Rintelen, former governor of Styria, would take over as the new chancellor of Austria.

There was only one way to prevent the imminent Nazi coup, said Dobler. The Cabinet ministers had to be informed immediately of the intended attack. Only prompt action could now save Chancellor Dollfuss's government and the country. Dobler implored Mahrer to lose no time and issue a warning. Soon it would be too late.

Karl Mahrer sat in silence while he listened to the excited man's revelations. Perhaps he was still somewhat doubtful, but Dobler spoke with such urgency and conviction that one simply could not shrug off his story. Of course, Mahrer felt far from happy in getting involved. If this proved to be a hoax, he would look like a fool, even be dismissed from his job. On the other hand, his intervention might win high praise and promotion from his superiors. Of course, Mahrer as a mere collector of dues had no access to the heads of the government. But was not Major Emil Fey, local chief of the Heimwehr, a Cabinet minister? Mahrer himself had never talked to the great man but his immediate superior, Franz Hiederer, would know how to approach him.

While Dobler continued to implore him to act, Karl Mahrer made up his mind. Clearly, his country was in danger and he would not be found wanting in such a crisis. He had a brief vision of being decorated for exemplary service to his government. Then he rose and marched to the telephone booth.

2

The Rise of Dollfuss

THE MAN WHOM POLICE INSPECTOR DOBLER tried to save had been born forty-two years before, the illegitimate offspring of an agricultural worker and a farmer's daughter, Josepha Dollfuss. A year after the event, the girl married a farmer, Leopold Schmutz of Kirnberg in Lower Austria. The boy grew up on his stepfather's farm, a village boy like many others, with a distinct leaning toward the Church. At the age of twelve he declared that he wished to become a priest, and with the help of the local chaplain he obtained a free place at an Episcopal seminary. He graduated in 1913 and entered the University of Vienna. However, after a few months he decided that priesthood was not for him, after all. His stepfather was disappointed but did not object. Young Dollfuss wanted to take up the study of law, but then World War I broke out and he decided to join the Imperial Army.

At the age of twenty-two, Engelbert Dollfuss was four feet eleven inches short, and when he presented himself before the draft board he was mockingly told that he would have to grow a bit. Undaunted, he volunteered at another recruiting office and was declared fit to serve. Soon he even managed to be transferred to a famous Kaiserschuetzen regiment (Tyrolian Rifles) and entered officer candidate school.

From May 1915 until the end of World War I, Dollfuss saw service on the Alpine front against the Italians. While the Austrian army suffered mainly defeats on the Russian front, it fought with great tenacity on those rocky peaks along the Isonzo and in southern Tyrol. It was the last glory of an empire which had long been shaky prior to the outbreak of World War I. In 1917, for a brief period, victory seemed near when the Austrians, with strong German assistance, pierced the front at Caporetto and came within gunfire range of Venice. One year later, the Austro-Hungarian monarchy collapsed. Luckily, First Lieutenant Engelbert Dollfuss happened to be on a three-day leave in Innsbruck when the Italian front caved in. His whole regiment was surrounded and marched off to a prisoner-of-war camp. He took the next train to Vienna and found to his astonishment that the empire he had fought for had completely disintegrated.

The return of an Austrian officer was a very special experience, very different from the road back of Germans, Frenchmen, or Americans. Whether conquered or victorious, these found their country more or less intact. But the Austrian monarchy had shrunk to a small, impoverished republic, and the returning officers were greeted with scorn and contempt. The angry and disappointed mobs—the polite Viennese turns into a particularly dangerous beast when properly aroused—tore off the badges and decorations of officers and a popular song of those days ran:

> Who will now clean our streets?
> The fine gentlemen with golden stars—
> They will clean our streets.

Therefore, Dollfuss started his career with a threefold handicap. He was a short, unimpressive fellow, he was of illegitimate birth, and all his precious war decorations suddenly counted for nothing. Ambitious men are often driven to excessive zeal by such circumstances. Dollfuss worked his way through college as an employee of a farmers' union. In 1921, he acquired a German wife, while taking a university course in Berlin, and the following year he graduated with a doctorate from law school.[1] The next eight years he worked for the Chamber of Agriculture and made a name for himself as an agrarian reformer. In 1930, he was rather suprisingly elected president of the Federal Railway Board. It was a political appointment, since in the meantime he had become very active in the Christian Social Party, which even up to this day is the principal conservative party of Austria (now it is called the Austrian People's Party).

The history of that party reaches back into the final era of the Austrian monarchy and is closely connected with the name of Karl Lueger, the capable demagogue and long-time mayor of Vienna. He had been the idol of the lower middle class, a handsome, witty fellow, unscrupulous in his oratory. His anti-Semitism influenced a great many people, among others a derelict house painter named Adolf Hitler. Most likely, Lueger would have been horrified about the consequences; he was not really a vicious man and his tirades were not meant too seriously. However, they impressed Hitler, as

---

1. In Austria, a doctorate is the normal completion of law studies. An attorney is always addressed as "Herr Doktor."

well as the Viennese journalist Theodor Herzl, and helped implant in him the idea of an independent Jewish state.

Originally, the Christian Social Party had a definite program "to help little people." Later on it became more and more reactionary. After Lueger's death it lost control of Vienna to the Socialists and it has never regained control since. However, the party acquired a great deal of support among the provincial peasantry and it was quite natural for a man of Dollfuss's background to support it.

During the first decade of the young republic, the Christian Social Party was led by an extremely capable cleric, Dr. Ignaz Seipel, who skillfully restored Austria's financial position. He retired in 1929, and for a time the party was left without strong leadership. In 1931, Dollfuss was appointed Minister for Agriculture. He remained in that position for fourteen months. In May 1932, in the midst of a serious political and financial crises, he was named Federal Chancellor (Prime Minister) of the republic. He was still not quite forty years old and at that time the youngest head of government in Europe.

The Cabinet he headed rested on a majority of one vote in Parliament. On one occasion it was saved only by the timely death of Dollfuss's predecessor Seipel, who had been ill for a long time. A hastily appointed successor saved the day for the government. On another occasion, victory was gained only because a member of the opposition happened to be absent. Dollfuss's Cabinet was based on a coalition with the small Peasant Party (Landbund) and the Heimwehr.[1] The latter was more of a paramilitary organization than a political party, under the leadership of malcontent army officers. It commanded only eight votes in Parliament, but these were often vital to the government's survival. From the very begin-

---

1. Also called *Heimatschutz.* Both words signify "Home Guard."

ning, the influence of the Heimwehr on the predominantly Christian Social administration was quite out of proportion. By accepting the Heimwehr as a partner, Dollfuss became dependent on a fascist group that was aiming to destroy democracy. Though the Heimwehr was on the extreme right, it was strongly opposed to the Nazis. It represented a definitely Austrian brand of facism without pro-German leanings.

The main opposition were, of course, the Social Democrats, still the largest single party in Austria. Like the rightist Heimwehr, the Socialists also possessed a military organization of their own, the Republican *Schutzbund,* a workers' militia commanded by former officers of the old monarchy, who had turned to the left. Its commander was an aristocratic officer of the old school, General Theodor von Koerner-Sigmaringen, though since 1918 he preferred to be known simply as General Koerner.[1]

Since 1927, when a large riot in Vienna led to the burning of the Palace of Justice, the relationship between right and left had become more and more strained. The Social Democrats had their stronghold in Vienna, which comprised almost a third of the Austrian population, and in a few smaller industrial towns. This led to a certain antagonism between the capital and the provinces. The Socialists were not really a revolutionary party, though some of their leaders loved to use colorful language. Dr. Otto Bauer, particularly, the intellectual head of the party, delighted in thundering speeches, spiced with calls to the barricades and appeals for proletarian dictatorship. In fact, he was mainly a brilliant dialectician with no taste for violence.

The "Austro-Marxists," as they were frequently called,

---

1. In 1951, Koerner became President of the second Austrian republic. He died in 1957.

were great reformers and they counted a number of highly efficient administrators among their leading group. Karl Seitz, the mayor of Vienna, was a man of outstanding ability who worked with a team of first-class city planners, changing the face of the capital. With its new municipal apartment buildings, playgrounds for children, and improved social services, Vienna became a socialist Mecca. Due to the Socialists' reforms, communism never gained a foothold in Austria. A small Communist Party existed but was outlawed in 1933. However, the Socialists could not prevent the terrible economic crisis which hit Austria in 1931 with the collapse of its largest bank, the Creditanstalt. From that moment on, Austria remained in a state of financial emergency. By 1933, more than 400,000 persons were out of work.

Pan-German aspirations had always existed in Austria. Even before World War I a party which maintained that Germany, not Austria, was the true Fatherland, had considerable support. This party praised aloud Germanic virtues and preached hatred against Catholics, Jews, and Slavs. In 1918, an offspring of that prewar party constituted itself as the National Socialist Workers party.[1] However, until 1932 it remained a lunatic fringe without any real influence. The more respectable Pan-Germans formed a party of their own which called itself the "Greater German People's Party" and entered into coalition with the Christian Social Party. By 1932, this conservative Pan-German party practically disintegrated. The younger, more radical members became Nazis; the more moderate ones turned into half-hearted supporters of the Austrian government. Hitler's rise to power in Germany changed the picture materially. The Austrian Nazis suddenly gained tremendous support from the other side of the border.

---

1. NSDAP.

A wave of Pan-German propaganda flooded Austria and began to threaten the very existence of the republic.

The idea of a fusion *(Anschluss)* of Austria with Germany was certainly not new. Right after the collapse of the monarchy in 1918, a plan to unite the two countries was quite openly discussed. It is one of the great ironies of history that Otto Bauer, a Socialist and a Jew, originally promoted unification with the Weimar Republic. In those days, Germany itself had a socialist government. When Germany turned to the right, the Socialists gradually lost their taste for any sort of integration. In 1929 the plan was once more revived by Chancellor Johannes Schober, though in a somewhat different form. He attempted to arrange a customs union with Germany, whereby both countries would discontinue their import duties. The project was immediately opposed by France and its allies and had to be abandoned.

It would be a mistake to see in those attempts any particular predilection of the Austrians for the Germans. The reasons were always political and economic, depending on the momentary party constellation. Austria and Germany had certainly much in common. However, history often placed them on opposing sides. During the eighteenth and nineteenth centuries, Austria and Prussia had repeatedly been at war. The last time was in 1866, when Austria was decisively defeated at Koeniggraetz (Sadowa). The Prussians—commonly called "Piefkes"—were far from being popular, and even during World War I, when both nations fought side by side, there were frequent conflicts. The Austrians considered the Germans arrogant and overbearing, whereas the Germans called their allies lazy and inefficient. Diplomatic relations were far from cordial. Germany tried to buy off Italy in 1915, by offering Austrian territory. In 1917, the Austrian Emperor Charles I made secret advances to the Allies but the negotiations came to light and failed.

The Hapsburg empire was multinational. Patriotism meant loyalty to the ruling dynasty. The many nations living in that vast domain were united by the crown. When that empire disintegrated, the surviving small republic had great difficulty creating a common national denominator. It took another world war and a terrible disaster to teach the Austrians that freedom and independence were worth living and fighting for. The war also destroyed the claim that Austria was economically too weak to exist as an autonomous state. As it turned out, it is now one of the healthiest countries in Europe.

But in 1933, Austria was shaken by internal and external crises. The violent propaganda of the Nazis frightened the government. Only three years before, the Nazi Party in Austria had failed to send a single deputy to Parliament. But now, with unlimited assistance from abroad, they seemed a tremendous menace. A new parliamentary election was a frightening prospect. It is quite possible that the Nazis' actual number was smaller than many people feared. But to the harassed political leaders the danger seemed large enough to avoid any actual confrontation. Dollfuss was also very much aware of his shaky majority in Parliament. He resolved the question of a parliamentary election by, in effect, getting rid of Parliament—a move that may have been planned beforehand or may merely have capitalized on an unforeseen event.

On March 4, 1933, a vote of censure against the government came up before the Austrian Parliament. During the balloting one of the Social Democratic deputies left the room to obey a call of nature. A colleague voted in his place but marked the ballot incorrectly. Dr. Karl Renner,[1] the Speaker of the House, noted the irregularity and ruled that the balloting was out of order. There followed a heated debate and Renner laid down his office as president of the Assembly. His

---

1. Later President of the second Austrian Republic (1945-1950).

deputy, a Christian Social Party member by the name of Ramek, thereupon also resigned. The chamber became even more excited and the third president, for no apparent reason, also declared his resignation and forgot in the general clamor to close this strange session.

According to law, only the Speaker or one of his deputies could convoke a parliamentary meeting. As they had now all resigned, there was a legal impediment to a new session. Dollfuss could not possibly have planned this somewhat ridiculous incident. But he was alert enough to jump at this opportunity. Here, finally, was the chance to rule without parliamentary shackles.

On March 7, he published a proclamation which declared that Parliament had eliminated itself. However, the proclamation continued, the government was still in office and resolved "to secure law and order in these troubled times." All public meetings and demonstrations were immediately banned and the press subjected to censorship.

A half-hearted attempt was made to call a session of a rump Parliament. It managed to convene for ten minutes and was dissolved by the police. The large Socialist Party remained strangely passive. They could have called a general strike, but they contented themselves with verbal protests. They allowed their strength to drain away until it was too late.

Dollfuss, much assured, now began to govern by decree. His jurists unearthed an old, half-forgotten law, dating from 1917, which gave the government extraordinary powers. The era of democracy was over. The road was now open to an authoritarian form of government. For all practical purposes, Dollfuss's move amounted to a bloodless coup d'état. He hoped to find enough support for personal rule without elected representation. In those days, many people felt that parliamentary rule was too slow and often ineffective. The idea of a corporate state was much discussed. Its government would rest on appointed representatives of the various professional groups.

Logically, such a state could not be based on various political parties. It could only exist if the government was powerful enough to control all political activity. Monarchy would have been a possibility. It had deep roots in Austria and still a number of active supporters, especially among the older generation. However, a Hapsburg restoration was adamantly opposed by Austria's neighbors and might lead to foreign intervention. Under those circumstances, Dollfuss decided on his own personal brand of authoritarian rule.

3

Fatherland Front

DOLLFUSS WAS FULLY AWARE of the fact that now he had to strengthen his position at home and abroad. With the Nazi menace looming larger every day, he urgently needed the protection of a great foreign power. Italy was the logical choice, as it could be reasoned that it would much prefer the existence of an Austrian buffer to having a common border with Nazi Germany. At least in 1933, this argument seemed quite sound. Dollfuss went to Rome and received firm assurances from Mussolini. By his resolute stand against the Nazis, Dollfuss also gained a certain popularity in the West. Within a few weeks, the little Chancellor became one of the most notable figures in Europe.

Of course, Dollfuss was intelligent enough to realize that his hold on the country was still very precarious. At his left were the Socialists, who at the last election in 1930 had gained

44 per cent of the popular vote. To his right were the Nazis, whose numerical strength was difficult to evaluate but who were constantly aided and abetted by Germany.

A coalition with the Social Democrats would have secured the government a broad base, but both sides hesitated. There were negotiations, but they never got very far. Mutual distrust was great; the Socialists, constantly branded as "Reds" and "Bolsheviks" by the government, feared that they would suffer the same fate as their German comrades, who had most ingloriously been liquidated by Hitler. Dollfuss, for his part, did not believe that there was much fight left in his adversaries and hoped to ease them slowly out of their positions of power. In this he was encouraged by the Heimwehr and particularly by a man who would play a decisive part in the final drama: Major Emil Fey.

Fey was one of the most decorated officers of the old Imperial Army. He even wore the Cross of Maria Theresa, a distinction granted only rarely for deeds of extreme bravery. He looked the part of the military hero, a ramrod figure with cold gray eyes and a prominent chin. Fey was completely dominated by two passions: boundless personal ambition and hatred against the Austro-Marxists. His political ideas were vague; he was a soldier first. He commanded the Vienna Heimwehr. In the provinces, the acknowledged leader was Prince Ernst Ruediger von Starhemberg, the scion of an ancient and wealthy noble family and an eager imitator of Mussolini. He had a certain way with his ill-equipped soldiers, the kind of charisma which appeals to boy scouts. But Starhemberg was far too pleasure-loving to be taken seriously. He was not really trusted by anybody and was doomed to political oblivion long before the German army drove into Austria. Starhemberg himself had a rather low opinion of his own supporters. "A kind of Praetorian Guard," he later called them in his memoirs.

Dollfuss's own idea was the creation of a Christian corporate state, strongly resembling Italian fascism but with the full backing of the Catholic Church and a strange echo of the medieval Kingdom of God. If the constitutional charter of his creation, the so-called May Constitution, is read today, it seems an absurd mixture of tradition and hypocrisy. The document starts "in the name of God the Almighty from Whom all justice derives." The whole tone is definitely religious, visibly inspired by two papal encyclicals.[1] However, the popes had viewed the role of the state as benevolent and paternal. Under Dollfuss's hands it became a glorified police state. Theoretically, the rights of the individual were granted. But in practice no real representation existed except for various corporate bodies, all appointed by the government.

In fairness to Dollfuss and at least some of his supporters, it must be said that they tried to preserve their country's independence with the meager means at their disposition. Once democracy had been suspended, no other road than the creation of some sort of authoritarian system remained. Fundamentally it had to be a one-party state, similar to the fascist or communist pattern. The trouble was that the majority of Austrians had no great desire for such an organization. Nevertheless, Dollfuss succeeded in fashioning his "Fatherland Front," which was to lead a troubled life until the occupation of Austria by Hitler in 1938. He did his utmost to insert a degree of pride and patriotism in his creation and in this he was undoubtedly sincere. Tragically, his high intentions were accompanied by far less noble deeds. Dollfuss failed to see

---

1. *Rerum novarum* by Pope Leo XIII (1891) and *Quadragesimo anno* by Pope Pius XI (1931).

that before undertaking any sweeping reforms he had to gain the confidence of a solid majority. He chose to become the ruler of a hastily constructed police state.

Having secured Mussolini's assistance, Dollfuss's next concern was the relationship with the "German brother nation," which had recently adapted an even more ruthless dictatorship. Hitler's rise to the German chancellorship preceded Dollfuss's bloodless coup d'état by only five weeks. From the very beginning of his political career, Adolf Hitler had declared the reunion of Austria and Germany "a task to be furthered by every means." He had hardly been appointed Chancellor when he started to apply himself to that task. A Nazi victory at the polls was made impossible by the disappearance of the Austrian Parliament. The only road to power was violence, and Hitler immediately began to apply pressure. To his thinking, Austria was a recalcitrant province and its leaders traitors to his imagined "Thousand-Year Reich."

As a first step, one of his bullies, Theo Habicht, was set up in Munich as "Inspector General for Austria." His orders were to organize sedition on a large scale to overthrow the Austrian government. At first there were only loud and violent demonstrations, the smearing of swastikas on any available wall, and frequent explosions of homemade petards and tear-gas bombs. A flood of radio propaganda began, which depicted Dollfuss as the slave of the Jews, the clergy, and of foreign interests. The Bavarian Minister of Justice, Hans Frank, even had the nerve to attend a convention in Austria and to make a highly insulting speech against the government. Arms and ammunitions were constantly smuggled over the long Austro-German border which runs partly in mountainous regions, difficult to control. When the Austrian government banned Nazi uniforms and demonstrations, Hitler countered by forbidding German tourists to visit Austria unless they paid 1,000 reichsmarks for a travel permit. The idea was to ruin Austria's tourist trade and thereby raise discontent among those who depended on it.

By June 1933, the situation turned critical. The Nazis began to use real explosives and several persons were killed or wounded. Finally, after hand grenades had been thrown against a group of auxiliary police, Dollfuss banned the Nazi Party and all its organizations. 1,142 Nazis were arrested, among them a number of mayors and civil servants. Most of the leaders, like Alfred Eduard Frauenfeld, the *Gauleiter* of Vienna, fled to Germany.[1] They were eagerly welcomed by Habicht. Austrian refugees were organized into a "legion" and well supplied with arms and equipment. Frauenfeld began to broadcast invectives against Dollfuss, in which he openly incited to bloodshed and violence. Nazi supporters were issued manuals describing Austria as the Thirty-fourth *Gau* (province) of the German Reich. Soon the Austrian Legion numbered 15,000 men, who were permanently garrisoned at the border. Dollfuss had never wanted this kind of development and—though it was not known at this time— tried to unfuse the situation. But Hitler remained completely unapproachable, and all attempts for peaceful solutions ended eventually on Habicht's desk in Munich. Diplomatic contact with the German ambassador, Dr. Kurt Rieth, in Vienna, led to no better results.

In the meantime, the Western powers began to be alarmed by the situation in Austria. In July 1933, Britain and France declared "their serious concern about the conduct of the German government." Mussolini followed somewhat half-heartedly. He was not too eager to align himself with the

---

1. A *Gauleiter* in the Nazi hierarchy was a district leader with far-reaching powers. Such posts went invariably to Nazi stalwarts of long standing.

democracies. The whole demarche had no effect except that the Germans acted a little more cautiously. During the summer they had even gone so far as to drop Nazi leaflets on Salzburg and Innsbruck by plane.

A month later, Dollfuss and Mussolini met again at Riccione. On this occasion the Italian dictator advised his little friend to strengthen the influence of the Heimwehr, destroy all socialist influence in Vienna, and remodel Austria on a fascist basis. As Dollfuss was now almost completely dependent on Mussolini's aid, he hesitatingly complied and went home with a firm promise of assistance in case of German aggression. Italy also delivered some old guns and ammunition to the Austrian army.

Consequently, Dollfuss made a few changes in his Cabinet. Fey became Vice Chancellor and Dollfuss himself took over the ministries of Security and Defense. The rest of the year was spent in frustrating negotiations with both the Nazis and the Social Democrats. Another attempt to negotiate was made through the German ambassador, only to be foiled again by Habicht. A second one, arranged by two members of the old Greater German People's Party, merely led to increased hostilities, as Habicht not only demanded all restrictions against the Austrian Nazis to be removed, but made a bid for the position of Vice Chancellor. And the man was not even an Austrian citizen! For the time being, this extinguished every hope of any kind of settlement.

A few months later Dollfuss tried again. At that time he feared an agreement between Germany and Italy at his expense. Furthermore, his own partners in government, the Heimwehr, had secretly contacted a Nazi leader by the name of Schattenfroh. Nothing came of their efforts, but Dollfuss took alarm; he received Schattenfroh and made it clear that he was willing to negotiate. It was finally agreed that Habicht should fly to Vienna and meet Dollfuss at a private home in the greatest secrecy. However, shortly before the intended meeting, the Nazis started a new wave of violence. Dollfuss, getting cold feet, canceled the visit at the very last moment.[1] The whole incident—like so many others in Austrian politics —had a touch of operetta. The German Foreign Office had been informed of the cancellation and told Habicht that the trip was off. Nevertheless, he left in a private plane, but was recalled by Hitler personally while already over Austrian territory.

At the same time, negotiations still went on with the Social Democrats. Some of the Socialist leaders—especially Karl Renner—were not averse to a common front against the Nazis, provided a minimum of democratic pretense was maintained. This would have included a final session of Parliament, its dissolution, and the appointment of a new committee with a government majority. But Dollfuss refused; he was now bent on authoritarian government. Another proposal by Renner for a legislative council of state was also rejected. An effort to come to terms with the Socialist trade unions seemed promising at first, but ended in mutual recriminations.

While these and other contacts were still going on, the suppression of leftist activities became more severe. The Socialist party organ was banned and the police began hunting for arms and ammunition of the Republican *Schutzbund.* The organized workers became more and more embittered, both about the Dollfuss-Fey government and their own leadership, which always seemed to temporize and hesitate. Their chiefs

---

1. Dollfuss's decision to cancel Habicht's visit was strongly influenced by vigorous opposition from Starhemberg and Fey. The Heimwehr leaders considered such a meeting incompatible with the dignity of the Austrian government. They were not far from right.

were indeed very nervous, and there was division between the pragmatists and the radicals.

Dollfuss himself must have felt very uncertain during those days. He was fully aware that neither his army nor his police force was in a position to fight on two fronts. He was surrounded by allies he could not really trust. He did not actually desire civil war, but was not magnanimous enough to let bygones be bygones and come to an understanding with the left. Instead of trying to unite his country against the enemy in Berlin, he attempted again and again to pacify brutal men who would give him no quarter. On top of everything else, he suffered lately from increasing deafness. He had narrowly escaped being murdered by some fool[1] and this may have strengthened his always present feeling of a sacred mission. His tragic error was that he permitted Fey and his clique to drag him into a bloody adventure that was to split the country for many years to come.

If Dollfuss, who by nature was not an unkind man, was frightened and unsure of the situation, no such qualms plagued Major Fey, his new deputy. For weeks he was busy working to disarm the Socialists, though he was fully aware that his constant searches for weapons could very easily lead to a final conflagration. But this was not enough. By the beginning of 1934, the Heimwehr started to purge the provincial governments. In Tyrol, the local governor was forced by armed insurgents to nominate men of the Heimwehr for various offices. Similar demonstrations took place in Graz and Linz, and in Vienna the government ordered all security powers to be transferred to the president of the police. So far

---

1. On October 3, 1933, a young man named Rudolf Dertil, a former soldier, fired at Dollfuss, who was only slightly wounded. Dertil was a lunatic without clear political motivation.

these had been the prerogative of the Socialist mayor, Karl Seitz, who protested but complied. It was now clear that events were racing to a dangerous climax.

A visit of the Italian Undersecretary of State, Fulvio Suvich, in January 1934, had probably increased the tension strongly. No exact reports exist, but Suvich almost certainly urged Dollfuss to liquidate the Socialists. At the same time, he seems to have secretly encouraged Fey to use all means of provocation to force them into armed resistance. The Heimwehr had long been on Mussolini's payroll and could be relied upon to follow the Duce's instructions.

A few days later Dollfuss appealed to the "honest leaders of the workers" to cooperate within his new system. It is questionable that this was meant sincerely; it may just have been preparation for a political alibi. In any case, the repressive measures against the Socialists went on. More ominous —but perhaps more sincere—was a speech by Fey, delivered to a group of uniformed followers on February 11: "Tomorrow we will get to work and do a proper job for our country!" He assured his audience "that Chancellor Dollfuss is our man," whatever that meant. The atmosphere in Austria had become so tense that a minor incident could lead to very tragic consequences.

4

Defiance of Hitler

THE FUSE THAT FINALLY EXPLODED the Austrian powderkeg was lighted by a man who was totally unknown to the public, one Richard Bernaschek, a local *Schutzbund*, or Workers' Militia, commander in Linz, Upper Austria. He had received information that government forces would undertake arms searches in Linz on February 12. This was probably the "proper job" to which Fey had referred in his speech. Bernaschek decided to use force against force. On the preceding night, the *Schutzbund* leaders in Vienna, Otto Bauer and Julius Deutsch, received a letter from Bernaschek, which was a clarion call to arms. It read: "Once our telephone message about arms searches and arrests has been received in Vienna, we expect you, workers of Vienna and all the working population, to give the signal to strike out." The message ended dramatically: "If the workers of Vienna leave us in the lurch, then scorn and shame upon them!" Bauer made a last desperate attempt to avoid bloodshed by sending a coded wire to Linz, but to no avail. On Monday morning police tried to occupy *Schutzbund* headquarters in Linz and were greeted by bullets.

At 8:30 A.M. the executive committee of the Social Democratic Party in Vienna convened to discuss the situation. There was still some hesitation about what to do, but the news of the fighting in Linz had got around and the electrical workers' union went on strike without waiting for further developments.

It was now too late for any compromise. The executive committee issued a manifesto for a general strike, but it was not printed. The presses could not operate because of lack of power. At 11:30 A.M., all lights in Vienna brightened and faded three times, the prearranged signal for the strike, then went out. Streetcars were left stranded and all electric power stopped. At first many people did not know what was going on.

The whole strategy of the *Schutzbund* was based on paralyzing the government forces by general strike. In 1933, when Dollfuss eliminated Parliament, a strike still might have paralyzed the country. But it appeared very quickly that this weapon had now become ineffective. Even in Vienna many services and industries kept functioning. Most important of all, the railways kept rolling. Years of depression and the long hesitation of its leadership had deeply affected the solidarity of the working class. Many workers were simply afraid to lose their jobs. They contented themselves with remaining sympathetic onlookers, while their more courageous comrades climbed the barricades.

The original plan of the *Schutzbund,* developed by one of its most capable commanders, Major Eifler, was to isolate the inner city of Vienna, which contained almost all important government buildings. But Eifler was arrested just before the fighting began and the executive committee failed to put his strategy into effect. In contrast, the government acted with lightning speed. All crossings and bridges were promptly occupied by steel-helmeted police armed with rifles. The military garrison of the city was immediately reinforced by Fey's Heimwehr. Numerically, the two camps were about evenly matched, but the government troops were far better armed. This forced the Socialists from the first moment on to fight a defensive battle. The morale of the *Schutzbund* was high, but as it could not take the offensive, there remained only one possibility: to defend its position with the utmost resolution.

With the failure of the general strike and without any semblance of offensive strategy, the revolt was actually a lost cause before full-scale fighting had begun. The government declared martial law and arrested systematically all Socialist leaders it could lay its hands on. Among them were Karl Seitz and Karl Renner, who had tried until the very last hour to come to an understanding with Dollfuss.[1] Bauer realized that all was lost and escaped to Czechoslovakia. Since he was more of a theoretician than a fighting man, this was no great loss to the cause, although it might have been more heroic to die on the barricades. He died four years later in Paris, an almost forgotten man. His colleague, Julius Deutsch, who was made of a harder fiber, carried on until the revolt had been defeated, then he followed Bauer into exile.

Though the *Schutzbund* had not achieved its objective on the first day of the civil war, the rank and file fought on with

---

1. Seitz was released after ten months. He survived the Nazi era, though he was again arrested at the end of World War II. He lived to see the rebirth of Austria and died in 1950.

unflinching bravery. It was now purely a defensive battle, concentrated on the large municipal apartment buildings. Some of these huge houses stood at very strategic positions and contained *Schutzbund* arsenals. These were not inconsiderable, though many of the arms were obsolete.

Dollfuss and most members of his government had attended a religious service in St. Stephan's Cathedral when the fighting started. Obviously, he had not expected that the Socialists would still be resolute enough to resist by force of arms. At noon he returned to his apartment close by the Cathedral, as it happened to be Mrs. Dollfuss's birthday. Allegedly, Dollfuss first wished to attack the workers' homes with tear gas, but it turned out that none was available. It was then that he made a decision which forever has blackened his memory. He called an emergency meeting of the Cabinet and ordered the use of artillery against the insurgents. Fey now took command, beaming with undisguised glee.

World War II and its unspeakable atrocities and the ferocious conflicts and repressions of the past fifteen years have somewhat blunted our sensibilities to such events. But such was not the case in 1934. The use of artillery against civilians shocked many people, especially in the West. The government claimed, not altogether without justification, that the workers' apartments were being used as fortresses. Nevertheless, they were inhabited and, naturally, women and children were exposed to the shells just as the armed defenders were. Besides, nothing even similar to that bombardment had happened in Austria since 1848, when Prince Alfred von Windischgraetz had also used guns to suppress a revolt. Apologists for Dollfuss have claimed that once the civil war was on, it was the task of the government to end it as speedily as possible. But the psychological consequences were graver than the loss of life which Vienna suffered from Major Fey's guns. From now on, to millions of Austrians, Dollfuss was the man who had shelled apartment houses. This was an action never to be forgotten and one is tempted to quote Talleyrand: "It was worse than a crime, it was a mistake."

On the night of February 12, half a battery of light mountain howitzers took up position opposite the Karl Marx Hof, a center of *Schutzbund* resistance. In the morning, Vienna awoke to the thunder of their guns. Fortunately, the number of persons killed was smaller than expected as the shells—mostly of World War I vintage—were of poor quality.

Though the Socialists were now completely encircled and outgunned, resistance continued until February 15. On that day, the Karl Marx Hof and the Goethe Hof, which dominated a major bridge across the Danube, surrendered. In Linz, Steyr, and Kapfenberg the *Schutzbund* also fought with great tenacity. In Steyr, a motorized Heimwehr column under Starhemberg had to come to the rescue of the hard-pressed government forces. There were other isolated fights, but in four days it was all over.

Those who had fallen on the government side were buried in a grand ceremony, with Cardinal Theodor Innitzer celebrating Mass. Their coffins were draped with flags and placed on gun carriages at the roll of drums. The dead of the *Schutzbund* were buried in a mass grave under police guard. No speeches or services were permitted.

Nine minor *Schutzbund* leaders were promptly court-martialed, sentenced to death, and hanged. One of them, a man called Muenichreiter, was seriously wounded and had to be carried to the gallows on a stretcher. In Holzleiten, an army unit executed several captives without trial. This and the imprisonment of thousands of workers gained the government the undying hatred of numerous citizens. No pious speeches and appeals to patriotism could repair the damage. February

12 caused a split which was to prevent any real unity in the country. The majority of workers did not desert to the Nazis, but they remained hostile, discontented, and aloof.

In France, England, and the United States, the press and at least some politicians were horrified. The little Chancellor, who had charmed so many people, lost a great number of admirers. As the West so far had done precious little for Austria, it is doubtful that Dollfuss cared very much about this. The Nazis were stupefied by the civil war; then they resumed their usual propaganda howl, now mainly directed toward the defeated workers. Mussolini was predictably delighted.

The government claimed to have lost only 128 dead and 400 wounded. The Socialists' casualties amounted to 193 dead and about 400 wounded. The actual losses among civilians were probably higher. The disappearance of almost all Socialist leaders—some in jail and some in exile—left the workers in a state of rage and bewilderment. A small number of *Schutzbund* members managed to escape across the Czechoslovakian border and were eventually given asylum by the Soviet Union. The small Communist party—it had already been declared illegal in 1933—gained some support but it was never able to build a strong underground organization. Dollfuss made an attempt to reconcile the left by appointing Ernst Karl Winter, a Catholic with leftist leanings, as third deputy mayor of Vienna and allowed him to hold meetings with workers, during which a degree of free discussion was granted. Winter did his best but could not win many workers over. He bravely asked for an amnesty, but it took ten months before the imprisoned Socialist leaders were released. By then Dollfuss was already in his grave.

With the Socialists defeated, Dollfuss now turned his attention to unifying the government forces and dividing the spoils of victory. However, his ally, Major Fey, who considered himself the true conqueror of the "Reds," proved to be a difficult man. There were even rumors that he wanted to depose the Chancellor. Dollfuss became suspicious and held Fey under surveillance. Besides, there was constant friction between Fey and Starhemberg, the latter, despite his weakness, being loyal to Dollfuss. The Prince still had a certain sense of chivalry and did not hesitate to praise the bravery of the beaten foe, a gesture which did not please Fey. Finally, it was decided to integrate the Heimwehr into Dollfuss's Fatherland Front. This gave, at least to the public, an appearance of unity which was far from real. Fey continued to grumble, and a few weeks later, to his bitter resentment, was demoted to minister without portfolio. Another Heimwehr leader, Odo Neustaedter-Stuermer, joined the Cabinet as Minister of Social Affairs. The Fatherland Front became quickly a large organization. It soon had a million members, although a great number of them joined only because it was opportune to do so.

Having mended his fences at home, Dollfuss again turned to foreign policy. On February 17, just after the brief civil war, Britain, France, and Italy issued a joint declaration about "the necessity of maintaining Austria's independence and integrity in accordance with existing treaties." This was all very well, but Dollfuss now required stronger guarantees, and his dependence on Italy led to the so-called Rome Protocols, signed a month later. These consisted of far-reaching political and economic agreements among Austria, Italy, and Hungary. At the German Foreign Office at the Wilhelmstrasse, it was felt that this "agreement has an unmistakable tendency against Germany." The German ambassador in Rome wrote to Berlin: "Austria has received a new and conspicuous pledge for her independence." Dollfuss had now clearly shown the Germans that he had allies.

His next step was the proclamation of a new Austrian constitution.[1] On the same day Fey was removed from his office as Vice Chancellor and replaced by Starhemberg. The ambitious major remained a member of the Cabinet, but for all practical purposes he had lost his functions.

To Hitler all these events were extremely annoying. That midget in Vienna, that Milli-Metternich,[2] had dared to defy him! And defiance was a deadly crime which the Fuehrer could never forgive. That insane hatred against everybody who dared to stand up against his will would later drive him to decisions which were of immense consequence. It led him to the invasion of Poland and to the attack against Yugoslavia in 1941, which delayed the Russian campaign and greatly contributed to the German defeat at the gates of Moscow. Hitler simply could not book resistance of any kind without being driven to acts of rage. With his signing of the Rome Protocols, Dollfuss had signed his own death warrant. He had not always acted honorably, but in the defense of his homeland against a megalomaniac he was in his right.

It has been said of another Austrian, Wallenstein, "that his picture in history fluctuates, distorted by the favor and the hatred of the parties."[3] The same can be claimed for Dollfuss. Judgments run from "heroic defender of his fatherland" to "poisonous dwarf" and "butcher of defenseless workers."

---

1. See p. 22.
2. Klemens Wenzel Lothar von Metternich (1773–1859) was the leading statesman of the Austrian monarchy during the Napoleonic era and the following decades until 1848. He was a brilliant diplomat, but his extreme conservative policy led to a long period of repression. Milli-Metternich means a Metternich one millimeter short. That nickname, invented by Dollfuss's adversaries, haunted him during his brief career as Austria's leading statesman.
3. By the poet Friedrich Schiller. Albrecht Wallenstein (1583–1634) was Austria's foremost leader during the Thirty Years' War. A general of the highest ability, he was eventually proscribed by the Emperor Ferdinand II for suspected treason and assassinated by his own officers.

His tragic end has influenced posterity and made him a martyr to his cause. Dollfuss was most certainly far from being a saint. The working of his mind was calculating and opportunistic even when motivated by the most noble intentions. He acted with courage but also with shrewdness. He would happily have bargained with the National Socialists had they only let him run his new Christian state in his own manner. His piety was sincere, but he preferred to see the finger of God where it helped his political schemes. He liked to speak of his divine mission, a tendency he shared with Hitler. This often made him intolerant toward persons who did not share his convictions. In his private life he was a very pleasant man and strangers quickly succumbed to his charm and humor. His small stature made him the butt of innumerable jokes but at the same time increased his popularity. On several occasions he showed considerable courage, but he was not of a generous nature. In his attitude toward defeated adversaries he was a small man and not only physically. In his relations with friends—or people he considered allies—he was often strangely careless and gullible and this lack of firmness greatly contributed to his cruel end.

To those Austrians who were neither Nazis nor Socialists, Dollfuss had a certain appeal. His support came mainly from the middle class and the farmers, especially from groups with strong ties to the Catholic Church and to Austrian tradition. Many others, who did not particularly care for the man but detested the Nazis, considered him the lesser evil. Among those who gave him qualified support were members of the old Austrian nobility and many well-to-do Jews.

The severe economic depression of the thirties did not increase people's confidence in democratic process. Almost unconsciously, many yearned for a strong man, a "man on horseback" who would solve all their problems. They were quite willing to sacrifice a certain amount of liberty for economic stability. Those who had been impoverished by the great depression were often resentful against the parliamentary system and felt no great revulsion against authoritarian rule. For centuries Austrians had lived under a monarchy that can best be described as benevolent despotism. Democracy was not as deeply rooted as in England, France, or the Netherlands.[1]

As both the Nazis and the Social Democrats were now outlawed, the regime, by sheer necessity, became more oppressive. Many civil servants lost their jobs because the government considered them untrustworthy. However, it must not be assumed that the average Austrian of 1934 lived under a reign of terror. Oppression never reached the degree that it did in Hitler's Germany or Stalin's Russia. Austria had lost much of its freedom but not yet its character and independence.

---

1. The Austrian monarchy had been very slow in introducing general suffrage. The first election in which all citizens were allowed to vote took place in 1906.

5

"King Anton"

ORN BY POLITICAL TURMOIL, Vienna remained a stimulating, if not a gay city during those critical years. In fact, its spiritual and intellectual strength was far greater than after World War II, when it gradually turned into a beautiful showplace, living mainly on its past. During the thirties, Vienna had superb theater and opera, splendid concerts, and a late flowering of literature. Among the famous authors of the day were Stefan Zweig, Franz Werfel, and Jakob Wasserman. A musical show, the *White Horse Inn*, had its 700th performance a few weeks before the outbreak of the civil war.

Salzburg had its famous music festival with thousands of visitors from all parts of the world—with the exception of Germany, because of Hitler's travel ban. For the smaller resorts and spas in Austria the loss of tourists from across the border was a great disaster. Many disappointed villagers tended to swell the ranks of the Nazis, who were strongest in Styria and Carinthia.

Financially the country was in a bad way. More than 400,-000 persons were out of work and about 25 per cent of them no longer drew unemployment payments. The number of beggars in Vienna was frightening. The years of depression in Austria were just as bitter as they were in the United States, but in Austria they were even more threatening because of the permanent political unrest.

Into this struggling society the Nazis poured their formidable propaganda. Much of it was of the most primitive type. An Austrian statesman[1] once called anti-Semitism "socialism for the moron." No better definition could exist. Young persons, who could find no fitting work or were stymied in their jobs, presented a fertile ground for propaganda. Small businessmen hoped to get rid of their Jewish competitors when the Nazis came to power. Next to anti-Semitism, agitation against the Catholic Church and against foreign financial interests provided the propagandists with nationalistic slogans. These often sounded vaguely anticapitalist, proclaiming a "German socialism" as opposed to "Jewish Marxism" The original line of attack against all democratic institutions was dropped when Austria became almost as totalitarian as the Reich. From that moment on the full blast of propaganda was directed against Dollfuss. He was accused of a sell-out to foreign powers, of acting against the sacred rights of the German master race. Pictures of Dollfuss were sent through the mail with the caption: "I am a traitor to my people." Many young Austrians were influenced by the expectation of more and better jobs in the greater Germany that would result from a Nazi takeover of Austria. This explains the relatively large number of

---

1. Engelbert Pernerstorffer (1850–1918).

Nazis among students and professional men.

When the National Socialist Party was outlawed, it promptly went underground and systematically started to undermine the bureaucracy. There were a number of very active Nazis in the civil service.and—most dangerous!—among the police. The pervading climate of uncertainty also caused a number of persons to play both sides. Many joined the Fatherland Front and clandestinely kept some contact with the illegal Nazi Party, just in case! The events which led to Dollfuss's assassination would be simply incomprehensible had the state apparatus been firmly in the hands of the government.

The illegal party had no lack of dedicated fanatics. In fact, the Austrian Nazi Party produced some men whose names will always be remembered with horror. One of them was Dr. Ernst Kaltenbrunner,[1] an attorney from Linz, later chief of Hitler's RSHA (the Central Office for Security), probably one of the greatest killers in modern history. Another was Hanns Albin Rauter, originally a Heimwehr functionary, later turned Nazi, during World War II SS Chief in the Netherlands and executed in Holland in 1949 for crimes committed during the occupation. A third was Odilo Globocnik, who took a major part in the deportation of the Jews. Temporarily *Gauleiter* of Vienna in 1938, after the *Anschluss,* Globocnik was later SS commander at Lublin, Poland. He committed suicide at the end of the war. A list of such villains and sadists could fill several pages.

Like all underground organizations, the illegal party was not one single unit. There were different groups who sometimes followed an independent policy. There was an Austrian SA and an Austrian SS, which often competed against each

---

1. Hanged 1946 in Nuremberg as a major war criminal.

other. There were Nazis who wanted a violent revolution, and others who preferred a legal take-over, even a coalition with the Dollfuss government. And, last but not least, there were some politicians who were actually not Nazis at all but hoped to profit from a change. One such man was Dr. Anton Rintelen, mentioned earlier. A lawyer of German descent, formerly governor of Styria, and for a brief period Minister of Education in Dollfuss's first Cabinet, he was at present Austria's ambassador in Rome. During his long term as Styria's governor, Rintelen showed himself to be a strict authoritarian with rightist leanings, living up to his nickname "King Anton." In 1922, he almost caused a serious upheaval by willfully arresting several Socialist politicians. At various times he had ambitions for the presidency or for the office of chancellor, but he never succeeded.

A heavy-set, bald man with the brutal face of an aging butcher, Rintelen would go to any length of intrigue, even to treason, if it served his plans. The otherwise rather gullible Dollfuss must have had some premonition that Rintelen should not be too close to the source of power. He appointed him ambassador to Italy, a grave mistake, because in this function Rintelen was practically free from control and observation. By the beginning of 1934 he started making contacts with Habicht in Munich. The latter delegated his chief of staff, Dr. Rudolf Weydenhammer, to cultivate the ambassador. During the first half of that year, Weydenhammer was constantly commuting between Rome and Munich; he paid no less than fourteen secret visits to Rintelen. By spring, Habicht could already feel assured of having secured a valuable ally. Rintelen would be ready to play a leading part in a future Nazi putsch—if he were to be Austria's next chancellor.

A man like Rintelen would clearly be extremely useful to those who wished to overthrow the government. In the first place, he had never been identified with the Nazis. Secondly, as a former governor and minister, at present a diplomat and in close contact with Austria's most important ally, he would inspire a certain confidence in government circles. A pro-Nazi government under his chancellorship would not be devoid of respectability. Rintelen had close connections with the Heimwehr, and Dr. Walter Nagelstock, the editor-in-chief of the *Neue Wiener Journal,* an influential rightist newspaper, was one of his intimates. Winning Rintelen to the cause was the first step for nazifying Austria.

There were other politicians who, without being party members, were at least sympathetic to the Nazi cause. One such person was the former Vice Chancellor Franz Winkler of the now defunct Peasant Party. Contrary to Rintelen, he was no mere political climber; in fact, he had served his country honorably in the past. He considered Dollfuss a dictator and had opposed the dissolution of Parliament. It is astonishing to find such a man in close contact with the Nazis; but in 1934, more than ever, politics made strange bedfellows. It is hard to understand today that some men thought of Hitler as the lesser evil. The constant pounding of Nazi propaganda calling for the unification of all Germans under one flag bewildered and confused otherwise relatively sensible people. Besides, there were still many optimists who believed that the violence of the Nazi movement was just a passing phase. Once in power, those boys would calm down and act as responsible citizens. Strangely enough, quite a number of Western statesmen, especially in England, shared that opinion.

Habicht had decided that Austria had to be kept in constant turmoil. In the spring of 1934, the Nazi terror reached fearful dimensions. The number of acts of sabotage rose from day to day. At first, the Nazis had mainly used homemade explosives, which caused no more than glass damage. But now they started to bomb railroads, power stations, water works, and telephone centers on a large scale. Mostly the explosives were deposited clandestinely in some innocent-looking package. During the night of May 19, a number of rails were blown up, causing tremendous damage. A few days later, the city of Salzburg experienced a series of explosions. Even the palace of the archbishop and the theater for the yearly festival were damaged. Part of that campaign of terror was purposely directed toward places frequented by tourists. In this manner the Nazis hoped to destroy Austria's tourist trade, which had already been hard hit by Hitler's travel ban. In June, the pressure line of the Spullersee power station in Tyrol blew up and a number of other utility plants were severely damaged. Attacks on members of the armed forces also multiplied. Large quantities of explosives were constantly smuggled over the border. In the frontier town of Kufstein, the police found 120 pounds of explosives in the possession of a German citizen after an act of sabotage had been committed against the local water-supply system. During May and June, not a day passed without new outrages. In Lower Austria, the entire telephone system was completely dislocated by hundreds of well-coordinated actions.

While this wave of terror was in full swing, Hitler paid his first visit to Mussolini. The secret records of those talks are now available, and they reveal a proposal which Hitler presented to his host. This German plan piously rejected the idea of official *Anschluss* as not feasible internationally. But it stated that compromise with Dollfuss was impossible and that he should therefore be replaced by a "neutral person."[1] This new chancellor would then call for elections. These, according to Hitler, would lead to Nazi victory and the Austrian

---

1. No name was mentioned by Hitler, but he must have had Rintelen in mind.

National Socialists would then take part in a new government. Mussolini replied that such a program could only be considered after a period of internal peace. Under the present conditions, no negotiations were possible. Dollfuss, said Mussolini, desired an agreement with the Reich and was merely defending himself. As the German ambassador noted, "There was evident divergence of opinion" between the two fascist dictators. The conflict was glossed over by a German communiqué but it persisted for the time being. Mussolini was not yet ready to abandon his little satellite.

Ironically, Dollfuss and his friends would have been willing to compromise, as Dollfuss's previous contact with Habicht clearly indicated. But Habicht refused to be appeased and the illegal Nazi Party was now being run by a number of desperadoes, who tried to outdo each other in radicalism.

Already in 1933, Dollfuss had been forced to take sharp measures against his opponents on the right. At Woellersdorf in Lower Austria, a camp was erected for political internees. It was not as bad as the German concentration camps, but the fact remained that citizens were put behind barbed wire without trial and for purely political reasons.[1] But even now the government hesitated to use capital punishment against Nazi saboteurs. There was still hope that Hitler would finally relent or be too preoccupied by difficulties within the Reich.

Those who still had illusions about the true nature of national socialism received a rude shock on June 30, 1934, when Hitler suddenly struck at his own unruly SA and had about 400 persons dispatched in a singularly brutal blood purge. Ernst Roehm, a long-time intimate of Hitler, and several other prominent SA officers were executed without trial for

---

1. Not all prisoners at Woellersdorf were Nazis. There was also a number of Socialists among the inmates.

alleged sedition. Very soon this type of gangsterdom was to erupt in Austria too.

The treatment of the Austrian question by the Germans during those critical months produced a sort of political schizophrenia, which was later to dominate the policy of the Reich. The German Foreign Office, under the guidance of the gentlemanly Konstantin von Neurath, acted with the greatest caution. The documents of his ministry constantly referred to the fact that all final decisions on that problem were reserved to the Fuehrer. A secret memorandum by Neurath's deputy Buelow spoke in very guarded terms about developments in Austria "which should continue to be given free play." Buelow was decisive about the fact that *Anschluss* was presently unthinkable. "German attempts in this direction will founder on the solid opposition of the great powers and the Little Entente."[1]

Lt. General Muff, the Reich's military attaché in Vienna, was confused about this attitude. He quite logically asked who actually directed German policy toward Austria. Was it the party or the Foreign Office? In a conversation with his superior, General Werner von Fritsch, he pointed out that any clear line was lacking. He even feared that Austria was becoming the rallying point of anti-German forces.

Indeed, it is obvious that the German diplomacy was hardly informed about the Fuehrer's plans. A truly grotesque little incident took place in Vienna only ten days before the assassination of Dollfuss. A minor Nazi leader by the name of Hans Koehler sent a memorandum to the German ambassador with a detailed plan for arresting the Austrian government. Koehler, who must have been some kind of simpleton, requested that his proposal be submitted to Hitler. The ambassador was

---

1. Czechoslovakia, Yugoslavia, Rumania.

horrified and reported to the Foreign Office: "Mr. Koehler was told by the German Embassy that the ideas contained in his memorandum were prejudicial to the policy of the Reich. In consequence, he was requested to prevail on his colleagues to desist from that plan. His memorandum has been retained to prevent it from falling into the wrong hands." The ambassador worried whether Koehler was still pursuing his plot in spite of all warnings. He recommended: "Appropriate steps should be taken to stop this action."

Indeed, the Foreign Office contacted Habicht in Munich and urged him to prevent any wild action of this type. From all that followed, one must deduct that the Wilhelmstrasse was strangely uninformed about what went on in Vienna and Munich. In any case, no instruction was ever issued to the German ambassador about how he should act in case of any violent upheaval against the Austrian government.

However, a document exists which shows the German Foreign Office and its pretended ignorance in a very strange light. On May 31, 1934, Dr. Gustav Otto Waechter, an active Austrian National Socialist, appeared at the Wilhelmstrasse for a conversation with Gerhard Koepke, director of the Ministry for Foreign Affairs. Waechter, a young lawyer and son of a former Minister of Defense, had recently become one of the most important figures of the illegal Austrian Nazi Party. To the German official Waechter explained the situation of the party in Austria with great sincerety. In his opinion, the future looked very depressing. The party was disorganized and disunited, several uncontrolled groups were working against each other. The acts of terror—mostly committed by the SA—were increasing aversion among the population. It was obvious that Waechter had no confidence in the SA. What was needed was one great final step, a violent upheaval to overthrow the Dollfuss regime. Hitler himself should speak the decisive word.

Waechter had hoped to speak to the Fuehrer personally, but he had to be content with a conversation with his deputy, Rudolf Hess. No record of this meeting has been preserved.

However, Koepke sent a report about Waechter's declarations to his chief, von Neurath, and the latter forwarded it to Hitler. It was filed with the remark: "Brought to the Reich Chancellor's attention. June 6, 1934." On that same day Hitler had a conversation with Theo Habicht. Here, again, we have no record of the meeting between the two men. However, it can be safely assumed that it was then and there that Habicht received the order which set the Nazi revolt against Dollfuss in motion.

6

SS Standarte 89

WITH HIS FUEHRER'S BLESSINGS, Theo Habicht could now effectuate his plans, which were supposed to culminate in the destruction of Dollfuss and his government. Of course, Habicht was well aware of the fact that no dictatorship, even a feeble one, could be overthrown without at least some assistance from its own executive branch. As long as that dwarf in Vienna was in full control of the Austrian army and police plus the Heimwehr, a successful putsch was hard to carry out. The Nazis had been secretly armed with weapons from across the border but they were certainly no match for regular troops. Habicht was not to commit the mistake of the Socialists: getting pinned down in a few strongholds only to be pounded by Dollfuss's artillery.

There was a fairly large Nazi underground within the Vienna police force, about a thousand men. It contained several higher officials, like the chief of the alarm squad, Dr. Leo Gotzman, and Dr. Steinhaeusl, a well-known criminologist. Two majors in the police force were also active members, and even in the chancellery itself there was a plainclothesman by the name of Franz Kamba, who was a traitor to his government. Even more important, the Vienna town commander's chief-of-staff, Lt. Colonel Adolf Sinzinger,[1] was a secret Nazi. Another army officer, Major Rudolf Selinger, maintained clandestine contacts with the Nazi group in the police force. The great majority of both army and police were good Austrians, but the presence of a few traitors in relatively high positions was an extremely dangerous weakness. The situation was to be duplicated on a far larger scale in 1938, when Austria finally collapsed. It was also repeated later on, in other countries, when disloyal officers or civil servants paved the way for the invader. Best known is the case of the Norwegian Major Vidkun Quisling,[2] whose name will forever be synonymous with treason.

Some of the disloyal police officers had already planned a plot against Dollfuss in 1933. It did not receive German approval and remained only a project. However, at the beginning of 1934, the illegal party made a very important decision. It formed a secret striking force, the SS Standarte 89. The black-shirted SS *(Schutzstaffel)*,[3] later the scourge of Europe, had only been a small military wing of the Austrian Nazi Party. The majority of young members flocked instead to the brown-shirted SA *(Sturmabteilung)*, which was responsible for most of the terror acts committed in Austria. The nucleus of the SS Standarte 89 was a group of Austrian soldiers, who had origi-

---

1. This man was involved in the plot against Hitler in 1944. However, there is no indication that he was ever anything else but a convinced National Socialist.
2. Executed for treason in 1945.
3. Originally, the SS was an elite guard for the protection of the Fuehrer.

nally formed a sort of Nazi cell within the Austrian army. In 1933, these men were expelled from the armed forces but stuck together under the leadership of a certain Fridolin Glass. They adopted the name of "Militaerstandarte" and refused to be integrated into the SA, which was a conglomerate of ruffians and bully boys. They preferred to make contact with Heinrich Himmler, the German SS chief, and were promptly accepted into his organization.

Here was the perfect instrument for violent action which Dr. Waechter had recommended to the Wilhelmstrasse. Of the men of the SS Standarte 89, most had been in military service and some still served in the police. Almost all had at least some training and ability to handle military equipment. Several of the older men had served in World War I. One of them, Otto Planetta, of whom we shall hear more later, had been a private in the same regiment as Dollfuss, though there is no indication that the two ever met until the day they came face to face in the chancellery. Another leading member, Paul Hudl, had served as a first lieutenant in the Imperial army.

The decision to use SS Standarte 89 as the striking arm of the Nazi revolt was made in Zurich on June 25. On that day Theo Habicht and his chief of staff, Rudolf Weydenhammer, conferred with two Austrian Nazis who were to play a leading part in the uprising: Dr. Gustav Waechter, who had recently intervened at the German Foreign Office, and Fridolin Glass, commander of the "Militaerstandarte." In the secrecy of a hotel room a plan was developed which logistically must be considered a masterpiece. That it failed was owing less to faulty planning than to a strange mixture of betrayal, sloppiness, and unforeseen incidents. It seems that most of the plan was developed by Waechter, who was undoubtedly its organizer and guiding spirit.

The plot envisaged the paralysis of the Austrian government with three bold strokes, which were to coincide. The whole Cabinet was to be arrested by the main force of SS Standarte 89 at the chancellery. The President of Austria, Wilhelm Miklas, would be imprisoned at the same time. A task force was to occupy the central radio station[1] and announce that the government had resigned and Dr. Rintelen had been appointed Chancellor. The whole action in Vienna was later given the code name "Operation Summer Festival." Once it had succeeded, a nationwide uprising would take place all over the country under the code name "Operation Price Shooting." Naturally, the success of the second action depended entirely on the progress of the first. Once a friendly government was established in Vienna, the take-over in the provinces would be easy. If the coup d'état in the capital failed, the provincial revolt was doomed. The Nazis could never hope to vanquish the by now fairly well-equipped Austrian army.

Logically, a relatively smooth change-over was absolutely vital and this was the role reserved for Rintelen. If he could assert himself promptly, if all the armed forces would obey his orders, victory was almost certain. By arresting the Cabinet and the President, a total power vacuum would occur and Rintelen would have to move into it quickly. With all ministries in the hands of Nazi supporters, resistance would have little chance to develop. The Austrian army was not used to acting independently and could be persuaded to accept the new government.

Most likely, Habicht explained to his Austrian allies, the military and diplomatic forces of the Reich would not go into

---

1. The Ravag Building in the center of Vienna. It was the only broadcasting station in the capital and completely controlled by the federal government. Its possession meant total control of all radio channels in Austria.

action. Officially this was supposed to be strictly an Austrian affair. Germany would supply arms and badly needed propaganda material from across the border. Perhaps some minor assistance from the Austrian Legion, deployed very close to the frontier, could be arranged.

Seen strictly as a design for action, the plan was cleverly devised and could very well have succeeded. It was based on the idea that within an authoritarian system a change in government—even a very sudden and drastic one—would be accepted by the population. The planners were in full cognizance of the fact that the Nazis in Austria were still a minority, though a sizable one. However, the Socialist workers, still reeling from their defeat in February, would hardly come to the aid of a government which so recently had used artillery to suppress them. The Fatherland Front, composed of divergent elements, not all of them reliable, could not be fully counted on either. There remained the Heimwehr, and here the Nazis may have hoped to make some kind of deal. It seemed not impossible to make arrangements with a man like Fey, who was known to have been thwarted in his ambitions. Perhaps some secret contacts did in fact take place, though no clear proof was ever found. If we may believe one of Dollfuss's secretaries,[1] Fey had even mentioned such contacts to the Chancellor. In a city so riddled with suspicion and political intrigue, crosscurrents ran in all directions. It was just the right atmosphere for desperate ventures and sudden betrayals. In one respect the conspirators miscalculated. The fact that they had some of their men within the military apparatus gave them unwarranted confidence that a good part of the army was really on their side. It was Fridolin Glass, the leader of the SS Standarte 89, who seems to have shown an optimism

---

1. Dr. Egon Krisch.

that was later on not borne out by the facts. The hope that whole army units would side with the insurgents was an illusion. It was mainly based on Glass's connection with the aforementioned Lt. Colonel Sinzinger and his associates. These noble warriors would undoubtedly have greeted a Nazi government, which promised more pay and promotion, with undisguised delight. However, they were not overeager to burn their fingers prior to its accession to power.

The second weakness in the plot lay in the fact that about 150 men would be required to execute the initial operation. A conspiracy which is based on the discretion of so many persons is always in danger of betrayal. Besides, there were a number of other people who were at least partially informed about the intended action.[1]

The meeting of the conspirators in Zurich was the first step which set the plot in motion. No date was yet decided upon. Waechter and Glass were told that their plan was a good one and that they should continue to find more collaborators within the armed forces. Weydenhammer once more departed to Rome to work on Rintelen. He did not have to use any further persuasion. Already on an earlier occasion, "King Anton" had declared his willingness to follow Habicht's directives, unconditionally. By now he had become impatient. As a diplomat he viewed the future visit of Dollfuss to Italy with misgivings. There was also talk of closer ties to France and a new guarantee for Austria's independence. Rumors about a new loan for Austria circulated. Should Dollfuss book more diplomatic successes, it would not be so easy to get rid of him. Rintelen was fully aware of Mussolini's interest in Austria.

---

1. According to one report, an SA leader named Kirchbach actually warned the authorities that Weydenhammer, Waechter, and Glass were dangerous. Waechter's suspicion of the SA was perhaps not unfounded.

More delays could very well destroy his chances of becoming Chancellor. Furthermore, Rintelen had arranged to take his leave in July. He would go to Vienna but could not extend his sojourn beyond the end of that month. The coup d'état should take place before that date. Also, Rintelen was doubtful of his position as ambassador. Transfer to another post might well endanger all his contacts. He now pressed for action. Habicht and Weydenhammer were willing to accommodate him.

Therefore, on July 16, another conference was held, this time in Munich, at Habicht's apartment on the Kunigundenstrasse. In the meantime, the conspirators in Vienna were assured of Lt. Colonel Sinzinger's active support. He did not appear at the meeting but sent as his deputy a certain Major Egert, decoding expert at the Austrian Department of Defense, as his deputy. Present were also Alfred Eduard Frauenfeld, the former *Gauleiter* of Vienna, now in exile, and Hermann Reschny, head of the Austrian SA. Glass reported on his army and police contacts and it was now decided that the revolt would be prepared for July 24.

One of the reasons why the conspirators did not wish to delay their action any longer was a new law, enacted by the Austrian government on July 14, stipulating the death penalty for possession of arms and explosives. Executions of National Socialists were now a distinct possibility. Such executions could easily trigger local uprisings which would be suppressed if the government remained in firm control. The Austrian Nazis would then be faced with defeat and disintegration.

Seen strictly from the German point of view, the operation seemed very promising. Once the Dollfuss government had fallen, the new regime would be strongly dependent on Nazi support, even if Rintelen and perhaps other Cabinet members were not officially connected with the National Socialist Party.[1] For the time being it would be sufficient to lay hands on the vital portfolios. Once the army and the police were under firm Nazi leadership, the remaining ministries would gradually follow. In this respect the German National Socialists were not without experience. It must be remembered that Hitler's first Cabinet was by no means a purely Nazi government. In fact, in Germany, when the Nazis came to power, they held only three of the eleven ministries. But within a very short time the non-Nazis were kicked out or transferred to offices where they were virtually powerless. The few leftovers —like the Minister of Foreign Affairs, von Neurath—promptly turned into obedient servants of the regime. A similar development was expected in Austria.

In the meantime, the hate propaganda against Dollfuss went on full blast. Night after night, Frauenfeld, now broadcasting from Munich, incited his followers in Austria to overthrow the government. The tone of those broadcasts was abusive to a degree unheard of among civilized nations. On several occasions the invective became sheer incitement to murder. The Austrian government had no means of stopping these diatribes, and the Germans completely ignored protests.

Dollfuss himself sensed the seriousness of the situation. He seems to have been especially alarmed by Hitler's blood purge of his own SA and the ease of his sordid triumph. As a kind of side show, the Nazis had also assassinated the former German Reich Chancellor General Kurt von Schleicher, the previous Bavarian state commissioner Gustav von Kahr, the

---

1. Long after the revolt had failed, a Viennese newspaper published a list of Rintelen's putsch Cabinet. It consisted of five non-Nazis, including Rintelen and Winkler, and six National Socialists. However, the authenticity of the list is doubtful.

Catholic leader Erich Klausener, and a number of other politicians who had nothing to do with the alleged SA revolt. Even to the most naïve observer it was obvious that the Fuehrer had not the slightest hesitation to liquidate persons who for one reason or another aroused his anger. Von Kahr, for example, had opposed Hitler in 1923 but had long since retired from politics.

On July 11—just two weeks before the Nazi putsch—Dollfuss reorganized his Cabinet. While he himself took over the departments of Defense and Security, he appointed as his respective state secretaries two men who were his trusted paladins. The Defense post went to General Wilhelm Zehner, a completely reliable army officer. State Secretary of Security became Baron Erwin Karwinsky, a man in whom Dollfuss placed the greatest confidence. The Ministry of Education went to the former Minister of Justice, Kurt von Schuschnigg, a very able young attorney from Innsbruck, a man whose high intellect seemed to make him particularly suitable for that office. As fate willed it, he was to remain in that post for only two weeks and then to his own surprise found himself the new ruler of Austria. Fey remained minister without portfolio with some very indefinite functions. He was now practically powerless, as Dollfuss had serious doubts about his loyalty and was having him constantly watched by plainclothesmen.

Suspicion of Fey had even spread abroad. Prince Starhemberg, visiting Budapest, was told by Prime Minister Gyula Gömbös that Fey was not to be trusted.[1] The Hungarian also told Starhemberg bluntly that he considered Austrian security measures quite insufficient and warned him of the consequences. Seemingly, the Hungarian intelligence service had some information that Vienna had not. On his return, Star-

---

1. Fey had recently been in Budapest and seems to have raised Gömbös's suspicion.

hemberg passed Gömbös's warnings on to Dollfuss, but nothing was done about it. Eventually Starhemberg, who was not much given to worrying, went happily on vacation to Italy. Dollfuss, though at least nominally Minister of Security, paid scant attention to any detail work in that department. In fact, as we shall see, the whole security apparatus of the regime bore a fatal similarity to certain comic-opera situations. The old sarcasm, that Austria was governed by despotism mitigated by sloppiness, was as true of Dollfuss's authoritarian state as it was of the old monarchy. In more than one sense the coming events were a comedy of errors—spattered with blood.

7

"Operation Summer Festival"

IN 1906, A FORMER CONVICT by the name of Wilhelm Voigt bought himself a captain's old uniform in a pawnshop. He put it on, then stopped a few soldiers, marched them to the city hall in the town of Koepenick, Prussia, arrested the mayor, and confiscated the municipal funds. While the city fathers sat trembling, the false captain quietly walked off with the money. He became known as the "Captain of Koepenick," and the incident was considered characteristic of German awe and subservience toward anybody in uniform. The story was later made into a play and a movie.

We do not know if that story inspired the men who planned "Operation Summer Festival." In any case, it was the same idea. A rebel force, disguised in army uniforms, would be aimed against the center of government to arrest the Cabinet. The plan was particularly tempting at a period when all kinds of military and paramilitary formations were a common sight. Even if the disguise of the insurgent force was not perfect, it would not draw too much attention during a brief action. Of course, the planners were presented with two problems: about 150 uniforms were required, and the "military force" had to be assembled at a safe base, where the masquerade was to take place. Thereupon the men had to be put into action immediately. Also, the group had to be motorized and moved quickly to its destination. Trucks, loaded with troops—even in none too correct uniforms—were not likely to be stopped. Of course, long rides had to be avoided. The point of assembly should not be very far from the seat of government.

The original plan of the conspirators was to assemble their "troops" at the headquarters of the Vienna garrison. This was certainly an excellent idea, as in a military building a number of soldiers—phony or genuine—was nothing unusual. Besides, it was at the headquarters in the Universitaetsstrasse, where the Nazis's secret friend, Lt. Colonel Sinzinger, had his office. However, it would never do to arrange such a large-scale masquerade during office hours. After 5 P.M. it would be fairly safe.

Sinzinger had made vague promises that two regular army brigades would support the uprising. It seems that the conspirators somewhat optimistically considered this a commitment. Perhaps Sinzinger's brigades would have marched with the Nazis had the putsch succeeded. As it turned out, they did nothing. Another problem was transportation of the insurgents. There was no chance of obtaining army trucks, but a Nazi industrialist was willing to provide the required vehicles. A military transport by private motor trucks—some with the name of the company that owned them!—would look a little awkward. But here again the conspirators correctly figured that it would not matter on a ride of about one mile. In case some policeman did notice the strange motorcade, the trucks would arrive at their destination prior to his alarm signals. The arms and uniforms—mostly stolen—were available. Here, too, one had to improvise. Some rifles had no straps; the men would simply have to carry them by cords, which were slung around their shoulders.

The final preparations for the coup d'état began on July 23. Rintelen had taken up lodgings at the Hotel Imperial, then as now Vienna's most elegant hotel. Habicht stayed in Munich and delegated the command to his ADC Rudolf Weydenhammer, who arrived in Vienna with a forged British passport. The rebels knew that the final meeting of the Cabinet prior to its summer recess would take place in the afternoon of July 24. On the evening before, Weydenhammer and Waechter sat in the office of another party member, the attorney Hans Blaschke,[1] who had been instrumental in procuring the badly needed trucks. There was little time to lose. A most urgent and unexpected problem had suddenly turned up. Wilhelm Miklas, Federal President of Austria, had prematurely left the capital for his holiday in Velden, Carinthia. According to the original plan, the President would have been apprehended in Vienna, at the same time as his Cabinet. Now it became necessary to send a small task force to Carinthia. The conspirators clearly saw that Miklas had to be put out of action at all costs. He was not the kind of man to sanction an illegally constituted government. Therefore, a man named Grillmayer, known for his daring, was chosen to start for Velden with several aides and arrest the President. As it turned out, Grillmayer was a most unlucky choice.

Weydenhammer's next appointment was with Fridolin

---

1. During the German occupation of Austria Blaschke became deputy mayor of Vienna.

Glass, the leader of SS Standarte 89, and his military allies. That meeting took place at Klosterneuburg, a small town on the Danube, only four miles from the capital. It is rightly famous for its medieval abbey, but the gentlemen had not gone there to admire art treasures. They met secretly near the local swim bath. Sinzinger and two of his subordinates were present. The location was well chosen for the occasion, as it was now evening and at that late hour the shore of the river was quiet and not much frequented. After their conference with the military, Weydenhammer and Glass drove back to the suburb of Nussdorf and met Waechter at one of those cozy little inns that dispense new wine. It was certainly the most unlikely spot for conspirators. Such inns are mostly visited by people who want a carefree evening with drinks and music. Even in the unlikely case that the three putsch leaders would have been seen by chance acquaintances, the subject of their talks would not have been suspected. In the meantime, the troop of future insurgents had been ordered to the Klosterneuburg swim bath for inspection. This was held by Weydenhammer and his friends late at night in the locker room of that establishment. The last details were discussed. Though Glass was the commander of the total operation, the striking force against the chancellery was to be headed by one of his lieutenants, Franz Holzweber, a bespectacled young man, who fancied a mustache like his Fuehrer's. For the occasion, Holzweber was going to wear officer's uniform and call himself "Captain Friedrich." The men were told that a new government under Rintelen would take over immediately after capture of the chancellery building. The final orders were to be issued just before the force went into action. Hands were raised, and Hitler was duly hailed. Then Weydenhammer drove back to the Imperial for further discussion with Rintelen.

The hopeful Chancellor-to-be had, in the meantime, talked to several members of the government, especially with the Minister of Finance, Dr. Karl Buresch, who was not one of the conspirators but on friendly terms with Rintelen. He had also seen Dr. Schuschnigg, perhaps in the hope of canvassing his feelings regarding a change in government. Had the putsch succeeded, Rintelen would almost certainly have tried to get a few men of known patriotism and reputation into his new Cabinet. A definite prospect was Dollfuss's enemy, the former Vice Chancellor Winkler, who was now entrusted with a diplomatic mission to Prague. Rintelen wished him to assure the Czechoslovakian government of the respectability of the new administration. It is doubted whether Winkler would have been very successful in case the uprising had succeeded. The fact that he was willing to undertake so strange an errand proved that he was deeply involved in the plot in spite of his solid democratic record.

After Weydenhammer had finished with Rintelen, he proceeded to still another restaurant in order to instruct the small task force that was ready to depart for Velden to arrest President Miklas. It was 4 A.M. when he finally got to his hotel room. The preparation for the overthrow of the Austrian government seemed now complete. He cannot have slept more than three hours, if he slept at all, because at 8 A.M. he met Winkler at his private apartment near City Hall. Rintelen, too, was present, and with much encouragement from the two gentlemen Winkler left for his journey to Prague.[1] The meeting of the Cabinet was scheduled for the same afternoon, and consequently the SS force was to attack the chancellery at 5:45 P.M. But as if fate wanted to give Dollfuss another chance, there was a sudden change in dispositions. It is not very clear

---

1. As the putsch failed in his absence, he did not return to Vienna.

what caused the postponement, but at 3 P.M. the Cabinet members were informed that the conference was canceled and would not take place until noon the next day. Did Dollfuss have any premonitions? Had he or another minister received any hints of what was being planned? It is not very likely because of the almost incredibly carefree behavior they were all to display on the next morning.

While the conspirators were getting their men and their vehicles ready, Minister Buresch called Rintelen and told him that the meeting had been postponed. This totally unexpected news was confirmed shortly afterward by Winkler's secretary and by one of the plotters, the police officer Kamba, who worked at the Ballhausplatz.

Rintelen was so thoroughly alarmed by this turn of events that he called Weydenhammer and suggested scrapping the whole plan of action. But he had not figured on the far stronger nerves and energy of his associates. With amazing speed and efficiency the underground apparatus swung into motion to postpone the operation. It was Waechter, operating from a café not too far from garrison headquarters, who calmly brought the intended operation to a standstill. It was now necessary to order all persons concerned back to their stations without raising any talk or suspicion, certainly no small achievement. The organizers, fearing that the sudden postponement was the result of betrayal, had to act with the utmost speed. By 5 P.M. they had the situation under control. Not only had the striking force been dispersed, but Winkler in Prague and Habicht in Munich had been informed of the new situation. The Velden task force had also been warned to delay action.

It was now necessary to revamp the whole plan because the circumstances demanded considerable alteration. This time the staff meeting took place in the private apartment of a

German official of the Reich's legation. This man was informed about what was going on, while his chief, the German ambassador, was according to all records quite ignorant of the pending upheaval. The official, Guenther von Altenburg, even assisted the conspirators in drawing up proclamations for the following day. They worked almost until midnight, then drove to Klosterneuburg to meet again with the leaders of SS Standarte 89.

As the meeting of the Cabinet was now to take place at noon, garrison headquarters could not be used as the base of action. At this time of day the appearance of so many men would have raised suspicion. Another place of assembly had to be found where about 150 men could change into uniforms, arm themselves, and mount the trucks for their fateful ride. Franz Holzweber, the newly appointed commander of task force Ballhausplatz, had a suggestion. There was a gymnasium adjoining military barracks in the Siebensterngasse, not very conspicuous and about one mile from the chancellery. Two policemen, members of the plot, would simply requisition the building. Each member of the striking force was to be supplied with a notice describing the place of assembly. At 12 noon the whole force would convene in the gymnasium and change into battle dress. Once the capture of the chancellery was achieved, Fridolin Glass was to inform Lt. Colonel Sinzinger who, it was hoped, would then honor his commitment and bring some regular troops over to the Nazi side.

The second action, against the Ravag Building—the broadcasting station in the Johannesgasse—was also carefully prepared. Fifteen men under the command of Hans Domes were selected for that operation. Two traitors in the Vienna police force were to assist the SS in gaining entrance to the building. The location and the interior had been studied but, as we shall see, the conspirators had missed one important detail which caused the failure of that daring coup de main.

The third group, which was to arrest President Miklas, had already arrived in Klagenfurt—fifteen miles from Velden— ready for action. And here, unknown to the leaders in Vienna, the conspiracy suffered its first decisive setback.

8

A Nation of Informers

SINCE THE DAYS OF METTERNICH, Austria had always been a nation of informers. Dismissed clerks informed on their former employers, jilted girl friends informed on their lovers, servants and maids were often used as spies by the police. When Austria in 1933 became a more or less totalitarian state, the flood of secret reports—reliable or not —mounted steadily. As both the Socialists and the Nazis were now outlawed, people with an ax to grind tended to inform on the political activities of hated neighbors or competitors. At the same time, rumors abounded. This was partly owing to systematic Nazi propaganda but also to the lack of a free press. Especially since the February revolt, newspapers were under strict censorship. Foreign papers, not hostile to the government, were still available. Of course, many people who had no access to them heard the news from readers who misread or exaggerated reports. All this added to the atmosphere of gossip and intrigue.

The word "treason" has always fascinated the Austrian mind. It dominates the dramatic work of Franz Grillparzer (1791–1872), Austria's greatest poet and playwright. His Emperor Rudolf, his King Ottokar, his King Alfons are always betrayed by friends and relatives. In a lighter vein, the poets Ferdinand Raimund and Johann Nestroy often show us submissive, treacherous valets who cheat on their masters under a mask of servility. Among contemporary authors too, treason and betrayal were a recurrent theme. Stefan Zweig wrote a masterful biography of Joseph Fouché, Napoleon's Minister of Police, a traitor par excellence. Three dramas in which treason plays an important role are Franz Werfel's *Juarez and Maximilian,* Schnitzler's *Young Medardus* and Karl Schoenherr's *Judas of Tyrol.* The theme of men betraying their friends also appears in novels by Werfel and Wasserman. The list could be considerably lengthened. Factually, treason had played a not inconsiderable part in Austria's more recent history. Shortly before World War I, the Austrian Chief of Counterintelligence, Colonel Alfred Redl, turned out to be a Russian spy and was forced to commit suicide. It was a most shocking affair with very grave consequences. For years Redl had supplied Russia with vital information on military secrets.

Now, in a period of plots and counterplots, the police were swamped with denunciations which sometimes turned out to be altogether false. In consequence, police officers, anxious not to be criticized by superiors as fools or alarmists, were often skeptical or hesitated to act on doubtful information. One has to consider that attitude in order to understand the following events.

Actually, the police had a complete report on the planned revolt on the afternoon of July 24. The informer was one of the prominent members of SS Standarte 89, Paul Hudl, formerly an officer in the Imperial Army and now in the lumber trade. Hudl had become involved in the putsch at an early date and was cast for an important part, which was to appear as the nominal, though not factual leader, in the uniform of a major. But on the morning of July 24, Hudl had second thoughts. He would have liked simply to back out but was afraid to be called a coward by his comrades. He decided to betray the whole plan, perhaps in the hope that prompt and determined action by the police would prevent the operation before it had started. Therefore, he informed a business friend, another former army officer, Rudolf Wurmbrand, of the revolt which was to take place only a few hours later. Wurmbrand was a member of the Heimwehr and Hudl knew that he would immediately pass on such alarming news to the police. This was indeed what happened.

At 4:30 P.M., a police commissioner got the full story and hastened to the station house to put that valuable information on paper. He then forwarded this report to his superior, who sent it to police headquarters in the first city district, which was responsible for the safety of the chancellery. The police detachment at the chancellery received that report in the evening. By then the attack had been postponed for the next day. The officer in charge must have thought the whole matter a hoax as the critical afternoon had passed without the slightest disturbance. The report therefore was duly filed—and forgotten. Incredible as it may sound, nobody even tried to inform the Minister of Security. The whole matter was handled in the time-honored bureaucratic way without anybody even bothering to make a phone call. Was it a case of sabotage? There is no indication of it. In that incident at least it was bureaucratism, not treason, which conquered all. It did not occur to any of those worthy officials to check on Hudl's information a little more carefully. While it was being properly filed and indexed, Hudl and his friends were getting ready for the final blow.

It had been decided that the insurgents would receive their final orders just a few hours before the start of the revolt. This was a logical decision, as it greatly decreased the chance of betrayal or indiscretion. And now we have finally reached the moment when Johann Dobler, police inspector of the sixteenth district, appears for a few brief hours on the stage of world history.

Johann Dobler had already been a member of the Nazi Party when it was still legal. At that time he had been finance manager of the party headquarters, the so-called "Brown House." It is certainly amazing that a man with such a background could still be employed by the police, but this was the way things were in Vienna in 1934. To the conspiracy, Dobler was a latecomer. On July 23, another Nazi policeman, Josef Steiner, had persuaded him to join SS Standarte 89. Steiner had told him that high police officers—among others the famous Dr. Steinhaeusl—were in the plot and that the army would support it. Steinhaeusl was going to be the new President of Police and would certainly appreciate Dobler's services. Dobler agreed halfheartedly, but the idea of denouncing the whole venture to the government must already have been in his mind.

Early on the morning of July 25, Steiner informed Dobler that final orders were now underway. During the morning Dobler was to visit the home of a certain Stephan Waas, Lerchenfelderstrasse 94. There he would receive written orders for action which was to take place at noon.

It is difficult to decide whether Dobler acted mainly from fear and opportunism or from suddenly finding his Austrian conscience. Perhaps all these emotions were present in the obscure person who decided to stop the revolt at the very last moment. As he survived his attempt only by a few days, we shall never know for sure why he eventually turned against his party.

Unfortunately, Dobler was not a very intelligent man and his first effort to betray his Nazi friends failed miserably. He was afraid—and with good reason!—that informing the police would not save the government but only earn him a bullet from a Nazi sympathizer. But instead of approaching the Ministry of Security or of Defense, he decided to call Karl Maria Stepan, head of the Fatherland Front, a known patriot and intimate of Dollfuss. However, the way he went about it was ridiculous. He tried to reach Stepan by phone, talked to his secretary and left a mystifying message: Dr. Stepan should immediately come to the Café Weghuber, where he would receive important information. Dobler did not even leave his name. He knew Stepan from photos in the newspaper and would have recognized him, had he only entered the café. But of course nothing of that kind happened. Stepan was told about the mysterious caller, but he probably thought the whole matter a hoax. Indeed, why should a man in his position hasten to a second-rate café to meet an unknown person who refused to give his name? Such calls were often made by cranks or practical jokers, and who can blame Dr. Stepan for ignoring it? Dobler sat nervously at his table and nobody came. Finally, in desperation, he decided to confide in a man whom he saw enter the café, the Heimwehr official Karl Mahrer, hardly the right person to alarm the government in a matter of life and death.

Upon hearing Dobler's story, Mahrer, after some hesitation, called his superior, Hiederer, head of the accounting department, who must have been deeply puzzled about a problem which so completely fell outside of his jurisdiction.

However, he showed a certain amount of common sense and ordered Mahrer to his office for a personal report. In the meantime, the unfortunate Dobler still remained at the Café Weghuber, while the hour for the putsch crept inexorably closer. Two other Heimwehr officers had arrived, First Lieutenant Schaufler and Captain Ernst Mayer. Like Mahrer, these two only wanted to drink their coffee in peace, but Dobler, getting more and more impatient, cornered them and repeated his story. Captain Mayer, who commanded a local regiment of the Heimwehr, was a more decisive person. He went to the phone and called not some underling but his supreme commander, Major Emil Fey, Minister in the Dollfuss Cabinet. Mayer, too, regarded Dobler's story somewhat skeptically, but felt that it might well have a real basis.

Meanwhile Mahrer, who had even taken a taxi, arrived at his head office. His chief, Hiederer, listened to the excited official's tale. What was the country coming to when deserving accountants had to act like heroes of a spy movie? However, Hiederer bravely rose to the occasion by calling Major Karl Wrabel, Fey's aide-de-camp known for his fervent loyalty to his boss.

It was typical that none of these men who had been informed about the plot made the slightest attempt to warn anybody outside of their own organization. They all acted strictly within the Heimwehr as if other government agencies did not exist. Nevertheless, at 10:30 A.M., a member of the Cabinet, Emil Fey, had finally been told that a conspiracy was in the making. He even got the story twice, from Captain Mayer, who had reported to him directly, and from his ADC, who had received Hiederer's version. Had Fey now taken prompt action, the revolt would undoubtedly have failed before it even began in earnest. There is no indication that Fey took the matter lightly. Quite the contrary. He considered it a heaven-sent opportunity to show his colleagues that Major Fey would once again save Austria from certain destruction. He would suppress the insurgents singlehanded with his Heimwehr and this time would not require any assistance from army and police.

To judge the matter in the right perspective, it must be explained that Fey was at present merely a member of the Cabinet without any command over the armed forces. Strictly speaking, even his own Heimwehr was subordinate to the State Secretary of Security, Karwinsky, much to Fey's irritation. However, Fey's own men were loyal to him and would follow his orders without question. But any order to the state police or the Austrian army would have to be issued through Karwinsky, General Zehner, or Dollfuss himself. Fey decided to handle the whole matter with his own military apparatus. It did not occur to him that in doing so the risk might be too high. His first step was to order Major Wrabel to investigate the whole matter and establish if there was any real substance to Dobler's allegations. This by now almost hysterical individual refused adamantly to enter any government building. He feared that the Nazis were watching every government office in Vienna. Therefore, Wrabel summoned him to the Café Central, the time-honored meeting place of politicians and men of letters, only a few minutes from the chancellery. Meanwhile, Fey went coolly to the meeting of the Cabinet which started, as planned, at 11 A.M.

Dobler was escorted to the Café Central by the two Heimwehr officers, in whom he had confided previously. Wrabel listened silently to the informer's tale, then made a rather sensible suggestion. Let Dobler go and pick up his orders for the rendezvous with the other insurgents. Clearly, Wrabel still had doubts about the truth of the matter. Dobler could have been an impostor or the unwitting tool of an even more complex plot. Perhaps the Nazis wanted to lure government forces to a certain location in the city, then deliver an unexpected blow in another direction. Also Wrabel, like all those who had listened to Dobler's story before, was worried about the brand of ridicule that would attach itself to an ill-conceived action. The Viennese are much given to mockery and there had already been several attempts to make the regime look ridiculous. In consequence, all higher officials—Dollfuss himself in particular—were much concerned with their dignity. Wrabel wanted to be sure that he was not starting a wild goose chase. Dobler and the two Heimwehr officers were to hurry to that mysterious address at the Lerchenfelderstrasse and pick up the written orders. If these proved authentic, they should immediately contact Wrabel. The three men took another taxi and drove to Lerchenfelderstrasse. The two officers waited at a nearby winehouse while Dobler ran upstairs to get his fateful papers. He returned with a slip which contained the following message: "89—12:15 P.M., Siebeusterngasse 11, Federal Gymnasium. Do not walk through Breitegasse into Siebeusterngasse. Steiner." The number "89" referred, of course, to the SS Standarte. The instructions regarding the approach to the gym, the base of attack, were designed to avoid too much pedestrian traffic. The sudden appearance of about 150 men, carrying parcels, could easily attract the attention of a policeman or an inquisitive onlooker.

The Heimwehr officers were now convinced that Dobler had told the truth and that a putsch was imminent. There was no time to lose. They ordered Dobler to keep his appointment, not to raise any suspicions, and hurried back to the "Central." As it turned out, Wrabel had already left the café and walked to the chancellery, just a few blocks away. His officers hastened after him and made their report, handing him the slip. Wrabel had now solid proof that something really serious was afoot.

It was now 11:45 A.M. Almost four hours had passed since Dobler had started on his attempt to forestall the SS revolt. And only now were the police called into action—though still to a very limited degree. Major Wrabel ordered two plain-clothesmen, attached to his headquarters, to depart for Sie-beusterngasse and to reconnoiter to see what was going on at that gym. If they noticed anything suspicious, one of them, Anton Marek, was to call Wrabel immediately at the chancel-lery. This was, at last, action, though these two men could only watch and report. Having sent them on their errand, Wrabel asked for Fey, who was inside at the Cabinet meeting.

By the time Fey received Wrabel's full report, it was almost noon. The Cabinet conference had been going on for about an hour. According to Dobler's orders, the men of SS Standarte 89 were to assemble at 12:15 P.M. Still, Fey's reaction was far from sanguine. His next move was characteristic, given his way of thinking.

It so happened that a Heimwehr regiment was going through a field exercise on that crucial morning. The training area was in the Prater, that vast area of meadows and swamps which stretches beyond the Danube Canal. Fey called the regimental commander, Lt. Colonel Pollaczek-Wittek, or-dered him to march his men into town and report to him at the chancellery. Since the troops were about three miles away it was obvious that it would take about an hour before they could be of any use. Only the lieutenant colonel and his staff were able to reach the chancellery within forty minutes, but their arrival did not help the government in any way. Again Fey had relied completely on his own political army. The regular Austrian armed forces were still completely ignorant of what was going on. As to the police, they were not aware of what happened right under their noses, except for the two plainclothesmen, who were now watching Siebensterngasse with mounting horror.

To add to the general confusion, the Vienna police had received a warning that the Nazis meant to assassinate Dollfuss when he walked home for his luncheon. He was in the habit of crossing Michaelerplatz at lunchtime and it was there that the president of the capital's police, Dr. Eugen Seydel, had posted a number of his best men. It has never been fully clarified where the information about that intended assassination came from. Perhaps a saboteur within the police apparatus had invented it. But it is also perfectly possible that it was just one of the many false stories and rumors that were constantly circulating. According to a later investigation by the German SS, such an action had, in fact, been planned by another group. However, it was canceled at the last moment and intentionally betrayed to the police, perhaps to cause a diversion. Whatever the truth, the chancellery on the Ballhausplatz was still completely unprotected, except for the so-called honor guard, a few soldiers with rifles but without ammunition. Their function was purely ceremonial and, because of an ancient decree, no ammunition was issued to such guardsmen. They could just as well have been the comic-opera soldiers from *The Gypsy Baron* by Johann Strauss.

9

The Closing Net

THE CONSPIRATORS WERE CONSIDERABLY MORE ACTIVE than
their victims, who for four hours had mainly made phone
calls. The Nazis had worked frantically until 3 A.M., re-
shaping all their plans. At 6:30 A.M. they were up again to get
the final orders ready for their troops. At 9 A.M. the three chief
plotters, Weydenhammer, Waechter, and Glass met for a last
staff meeting at the Café Eiles near City Hall.

Most of the action and counteraction took place in Vienna
coffeehouses. This might amaze people who are not very fa-
miliar with Austrian conditions in the thirties. It would seem
that the comings and goings in such establishments could be
rather effortlessly controlled by the police or their informers.
But nobody paid any attention. Only a very few of such meetings were held in the privacy of homes where close observation would have been difficult or even impossible. Waechter

and Weydenhammer, after giving Glass their last instructions, went to inspect the route which their motorized column would have to follow a few hours later. Nothing was left to chance. Satisfied that no detours or obstacles would hinder their operation, they separated. Waechter went to a restaurant near the Ballhausplatz, which was to serve as his observation post. Weydenhammer went to join Rintelen at the Imperial. Glass, the actual field commander, took his position at the gym on Siebensterngasse. The building was locked, but at 11:45 A.M. two Nazi policemen broke down the doors, pretending to search and requisition it. As such actions were by no means unusual, this went unnoticed. The base of operation was now ready to receive the striking force. At 12 noon, the members of SS Standarte 89 arrived as planned, among them Johann Dobler, who had just betrayed the whole enterprise, and Paul Hudl, who had done the same on the previous day. Both must have felt rather uncomfortable. However, Hudl looked resplendent in his improvised uniform as a major and, during the events that followed, showed no fear or uncertainty.

Some of the insurgents had donned their uniforms at home; a few were, in fact, policemen in their regular attire. The majority carried their equipment in ordinary packages, walked into the gym, and began dressing for the occasion. In the meantime, the two plainclothesmen, sent by Major Wrabel, had also arrived.

In all this mire of treason, halfheartedness, and inefficiency it is refreshing to report that at least one Austrian official acted with courage and common sense on that black day. This unsung hero was Anton Marek, an ordinary police officer, who for a few moments appeared on the stage of world history. Marek had watched the strange migration to Siebeusterngasse for about ten minutes. That something very unusual was taking place now became quite clear to him. At 12:10 P.M. he hurried to the nearest telephone booth and rang up Wrabel at the chancellery. He reported a brisk influx of persons into the gymnasium, some of them in uniform, most of them civilians with packages. Only ten minutes before that phone call, Fey had finally informed Chancellor Dollfuss that the seat of government was under imminent danger of attack. He left Wrabel in another room to receive telephone messages and walked back into the hall where the Cabinet was conferring. Fey took Dollfuss aside and the two men were seen to be whispering to each other. Dollfuss was seemingly doubtful about what he heard. He shook his head. But eventually he stepped to the conference table and addressed his colleagues as follows:

"Fey just told me something. I don't know yet whether there is anything behind it. But perhaps it's better to interrupt our session now. Every minister should return to his own department! I shall let the gentlemen know when we can continue."

Fritz Stockinger, the Minister of Trade, tried to remonstrate, but Dollfuss remained firm and dismissed the Cabinet. He asked only Fey, Karwinsky, and General Zehner to stay behind. He marched the three men into his inner office and asked Fey to repeat his statement. The major did so briefly: "I have received a message that an attack is planned against the Ballhausplatz. A gym in the Siebeusternstrasse is supposed to have something to do with it." It was certainly not a very illuminating speech. Fey had never been a man of many words, but it is amazing that he did not even mention the measures he had just taken himself. After all, a whole regiment of his Heimwehr was now marching in the direction of the Ballhausplatz. And not one word was said of the urgency of the hour, though Fey knew from Dobler's slip of paper that the insurgents were right now assembling at their base. It is not unnatural that Fey was later regarded by his colleagues with suspicion. However, there is no indication that he was in league with the Nazis. He was just playing it cool in the pleasant expectation of showing those gentlemen—especially that arrogant Baron Karwinsky—that Major Fey was the man of the hour.

In the meantime, a nervous Major Wrabel got Marek's first message from Siebeusterngasse and reported it to Karwinsky. This was now the first opportunity for the new Secretary of Security to take matters into his hands. He promptly called the president of police, Eugen Seydel, and ordered him to send a police car for reconnaissance to that ominous gym. He had hardly put the receiver down when Marek called again. His second message left no doubt about the seriousness of the situation: "Those civilians are donning army uniforms. Arms are being distributed. A truck in front of the gym is being loaded with various boxes and bags."

Karwinsky called Seydel again. This time the president of police was somewhat apologetic. He had not been able to send the reconnaissance car yet, because all available forces had been concentrated on Michaeler Platz where, according to rumor, an attempt on Dollfuss's life was being plotted. Karwinsky merely repeated his instructions. Perhaps he believed that the military guard at the gate of the chancellery was sufficient protection. He was not aware of the fact that these soldiers were mainly for show. Another fifteen minutes passed in uneasy silence. At 12:30 P.M. Marek was on the phone again. This time he sounded upset.

"Four more trucks have driven up in front of the building. Those men are mounting the trucks. There is no more time to lose!"

It was his last call, because the insurgents had noticed him and surrounded his telephone booth. Probably somebody had recognized him as a police officer—after all, there were several of his colleagues around. In any case, the rebels were taking no chances. They simply dragged him into one of their trucks and drove off. But Anton Marek was not one to be so easily caught. When the truck slowed at an intersection, he fought his captors off and jumped out. He escaped uninjured, but by now it was too late to send any further warnings.

After Marek's third call, Dollfuss ordered General Zehner to leave the chancellery and sound the alarm. It was Dollfuss's last order and a good one, because it gave his general freedom of movement. Within a half hour Zehner, too, would have been caught in the net that was now rapidly closing. Unfortunately, even General Zehner seemed to be completely oblivious to the fact that the building was still virtually without military protection. Even at this late hour it would still have been possible to block the entrance and issue ammunition to the guards. But nobody seemed to think of taking such elementary measures.

Karwinsky was now on the phone again but could not reach Seydel, who was probably hanging on some other telephone. However, Karwinsky was finally getting impatient and ordered two alarm squads to rush out immediately. One was to protect the Ballhausplatz, the second to stop the rebels at Siebeusterngasse. These orders could still have narrowly saved the day had they been followed up promptly and with sufficient police personnel. But either Karwinsky had been misunderstood or the officials who passed his orders on were sabotaging or simply incompetent. Only one motorized police officer was sent to the chancellery to observe the situation. A police car under police commissioner, Dr. Penn, did indeed drive to Siebeusterngasse, arriving just in time to see the departure of the insurgents in uniform. For a moment, Dr.

Penn took them for regular troops from the nearby barracks. After some hesitation, the policemen began to investigate the gym, and they ran into a suspicious-looking individual in uniform. When they stopped him, he pushed them aside and ran away. It was Fridolin Glass, the commander of the now motorized striking force. He had seen his men off and was just getting ready to follow them when he was intercepted by the police. Glass escaped, and, with notable presence of mind, entered a department store where he bought himself a hat and a coat. By thus changing again into civilian attire he hoped to mislead the policemen, and in this he succeeded, at least temporarily. Nevertheless, Dr. Penn's belated intervention had unexpectedly robbed the SS of their leader.

While all this was going on, Dollfuss, Karwinsky, and Fey were still waiting for protection from their armed forces. Fey was convinced that his Heimwehr regiment would arrive in time. The officers were already at the chancellery, but their troops were still marching into the Inner City. Karwinsky ordered the chancellery's outer gate closed, but this order was not carried out. It is not very clear if this was another case of inefficiency or outright treason. Possibly the officer in charge thought that order unnecessary because the guard always changed at 12:50 P.M. as a matter of daily routine. At that time of day the gate was opened and the relief guard entered the courtyard. This fact was well known to the rebels, who had timed their raid accordingly. Here, again, their intelligence work had been perfect and nobody in the chancellery had given thought to the danger that could arise from that ceremonious but totally unnecessary procedure.

We shall never know what went on in Dollfuss's mind while the last critical half hour passed. At first, faced with Fey's brief and incomplete message, he had acted with coolness and foresight. Now, eight of his ten ministers, among them the

Secretary of Defense, had left the building. The rebels' chance to catch the whole Cabinet with one single blow was gone before their trucks had even started to move. It almost seems that there were only two people on the government side who acted with good common sense: the Chancellor and that intrepid police inspector, Anton Marek.

There is one enigmatic question which no one will ever answer quite satisfactorily. Why did Dollfuss himself insist on staying in the chancellery? He could have saved himself easily by simply ordering a car and driving to the Ministry of Defense or some other safe building. Had he taken an unhurried walk to his apartment, chances are that he would have escaped his fate. The rebels had concentrated all their forces on the chancellery and the Ravag Building. They had no men to spare, and there is no indication whatsoever that they could have struck at Dollfuss if he had only left the seat of his government. It is strange that this simple idea should not have passed through the otherwise very clear mind of the little Chancellor. He had instinctively made the right decision when he ordered the ministers to disperse. Almost an hour had now passed; all reports indicated that the situation was deadly serious, but Dollfuss seems not even to have considered bringing himself to safety. Between Marek's last urgent message and the actual attack on the chancellery there was an interval of twenty minutes. Perhaps Dollfuss ignored the fact that the guards were unarmed. But even assuming that he thought himself better guarded than he actually was, what could a handful of soldiers have achieved against a rebel force of 150 armed men? What makes this matter more puzzling is that Fey had not mentioned that a Heimwehr regiment was on its way. How did Dollfuss, the nominal head of all security forces in Austria, intend to stop the insurgents, who were only a mile away, when he received Marek's first message?

Perhaps the answer lies in Dollfuss's personal attitude. He was certainly no coward and highly sensitive to the least slur on his dignity. Though he forced himself to smile about the many jokes concerning his short stature, he was actually touchy and hated ridicule. The mere idea of running away from a threat was probably abhorrent to him. Dollfuss was far from being a knight in shining armor, though some of his biographers have tried to glorify him as a sort of twentieth-century David slain by Goliath. Dollfuss was shrewd and ruthless when his interests were at stake, and in his dealings with the Nazis he was by no means always as principled as his supporters believed. However, he possessed two qualities which raised him above many of his contemporaries. He was sincere in his efforts to keep his beleaguered country independent, and he was brave enough to face personal danger. Perhaps one could say of Dollfuss what Tacitus said about the Emperor Otho, that in the eyes of posterity he earned about an equal share of infamy and of glory.

10

At the Ballhausplatz

THE FEDERAL CHANCELLERY ON THE BALLHAUSPLATZ was built in 1719 by Lukas von Hildebrand for Prince Kaunitz, later Chancellor of Maria Theresa and a sworn enemy of Prussia. The Congress of Vienna convened in the stately cream-colored baroque building in 1814, "to cut up the cake" of Europe. Three rooms on the first floor were used for that historic conference. During the later Hapsburg era the building served as Ministry of Foreign Affairs, which became identified with the name "Ballhausplatz." Under the republic it became the "Office of the Federal Chancellor"— in other words, the seat of the Austrian government. Today it still serves the same purpose.

One of the rooms, adorned with a large portrait of Maria Theresa, was Dollfuss's office. It was adjoined by the so-called "corner room," which has two windows, a Louis XV sofa, and

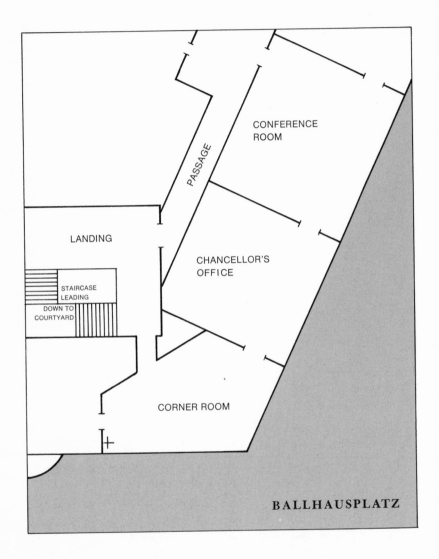

other eighteenth-century furniture. One door leads to the Chancellor's office, a second into another part of the building. The third room on this floor is called the Hall of Pillars and is used for Cabinet meetings.[1] Above and beyond, there is a multitude of landings, passages, and small offices. Visitors have often compared the chancellery to a rabbit warren.

Below, within the main gate, there is a courtyard from which a staircase ascends to the state rooms on the first floor. There are several small exits toward the rear of the building. Also to the rear was the office of the Federal President, Wilhelm Miklas.

At 12:50 P.M., as on any other day, the new guard detachment marched peacefully through the wide-open gate to relieve their comrades. At this very moment the motorized column of insurgents drove up, precisely on time, and simply passed behind the military guard into the courtyard. Their eight trucks unloaded a motley crew of "soldiers" in ill-fitting, pieced-together uniforms that could never have deceived a careful observer. More authentic were the ten policemen who took part in the raid. The so-called officers wore fanciful disguise, with Paul Hudl, the double-dealing lumber merchant, outwardly in command. He appeared as a major of the general staff, his chest decorated with medals. The real commander, Franz Holzweber, and another insurgent, Otto Planetta, were dressed as army captains.

In a moment the hapless guards were disarmed—a rather superfluous operation, as their rifles were useless anyway. Neither the few police officials within the building nor Fey's Heimwehr officers, who had arrived only fifteen minutes earlier, made the slightest show of resistance. The majority of the personnel employed in the building were driven into the

---

1. See plan.

chancellery yard, others into the few larger rooms. The female typists and secretaries were locked into the basement.

Upstairs, Dollfuss and his two ministers saw the trucks drive into the yard. Perhaps they too were deceived for a moment into believing that this was a protective garrison, sent out by General Zehner. But Karwinsky, taking a closer look, realized the awful truth. Then Major Wrabel stormed into the Chancellor's office, shouting, "The Nazis are in the building!" It was now 12:52 P.M. Karwinsky had a quick intuition. He remembered an abandoned cloakroom upstairs and, taking Dollfuss by the arm, said: "Chancellor, come to the third floor, you will be safe there!" He conducted Dollfuss into the Hall of Pillars. Fey and Wrabel followed. At that moment Dollfuss's personal attendant, Hedvicek, appeared suddenly from an opposite door. He pulled the Chancellor by his other arm and motioned him to follow. Hedvicek knew the building intimately. He dragged Dollfuss to the side door at the opposite end of the corner room. Through that door an exit to the Minoritenplatz at the rear of the building could be reached. Hedvicek's action was quite logical and it is highly probable that Dollfuss could have escaped in that manner. The rebels had no forces on the Minoritenplatz; they were all busy rounding up their prisoners inside the building. Dollfuss, trusting Hedvicek's knowledge, allowed the attendant to drag him back into his office toward the corner room. They reached the fateful door, which was not locked, but Hedvicek, in his excitement, fidgeted while the rebels were entering the Hall of Pillars. Fey thought he recognized the uniforms of his old regiment and shouted angrily: "You swine want to be Deutschmeister?"[1] He need not have bothered, for the uni-

---

1. The Hoch- and Deutschmeister were among the most renowned regiments of the Old Imperial Army.

forms were stolen. While some of the rebels captured him, Wrabel, and Karwinsky, a few others stormed into the corner room. We have two different descriptions of what happened during the next minutes.

According to Hedvicek, one of the rebels ran toward Dollfuss, who instinctively raised his hands to protect his face. The attacker fired twice from close up. Dollfuss fell to the floor and cried feebly for help. One of the intruders yelled "Get up!" but Dollfuss seemed to have lost consciousness. Hedvicek, who survived victim and murderer by many years, never changed his testimony, and there is little reason to doubt it.

When Otto Planetta was on trial for killing the Chancellor, he told a markedly different story. He admitted having entered the corner room pistol in hand but without the intention of committing murder. The Venetian blinds were drawn and he vaguely observed three persons in the dark. One of them turned and raised his hands against him, perhaps even brushed against his arm. At that moment he unintentionally pulled the trigger. Only afterward did he realize that he had shot the Chancellor. He insisted that he fired only once.

Planetta's version was repeated later by another insurgent, Fritz Lehrer, who had talked to him soon after the shooting. According to Lehrer, Planetta said even then that he had acted in self-defense. However, Planetta's statement is contradicted by Hedvicek on three different points. The attendant denied that the room was dark. He said that only he and Dollfuss were in the room when the shots were fired. And— most important—he declared that Planetta had fired twice. An autopsy proved his statement correct beyond any possible doubt. One bullet had struck Dollfuss on the left side of the throat but had not caused fatal injury. The second bullet had pierced throat and spinal column and left the body at the right armpit. Both shots had been fired from a distance of approximately six inches. The injury to the spinal column led to paralysis of the legs. As there is not the slightest indication that anyone else had made use of firearms, it can be safely concluded that both shots were fired by Planetta. It is understandable that Planetta—faced with a death sentence—tried to describe the event as an unfortunate accident, manslaughter at worst. It was his only chance to escape the gallows.

What makes it almost certain that the rebels intended to do away with Dollfuss is their behavior after the shooting. At first they left the profusely bleeding man lying prostrate on the floor. One of the SS men, Viktor Stiastny, unbuttoned Dollfuss's jacket because he had been told that the Chancellor always wore a bulletproof vest. He found to his surprise that this was not true. As we have seen, Dollfuss paid very little attention to his safety. Stiastny then calmly took Dollfuss's wallet from his coat and handed it to his commander Holzweber, who was just entering the room. It was later found on the floor, minus the cash. Holzweber did not comment on the shooting: he seems to have taken the situation in a matter-of-fact way and at first paid little attention to the wounded Chancellor. During the next forty minutes Dollfuss was left to himself. Perhaps the insurgents hoped that he would quietly bleed to death and thereby save them any further embarrassment. Finally—it was now 1:45 P.M.—the rebels asked their prisoners downstairs if anyone among their number could administer first aid. Two policemen, Rudolf Messinger and Johann Greifeneder, came forward and were escorted to the corner room. They found Dollfuss unconscious on the floor. One of his captors was sitting at his desk, smoking. About ten others stood around, watching the scene.

The two policemen requested that a doctor be called and were told to address themselves to "Major" Hudl, who flatly refused. However, they were permitted to carry the Chancellor to a couch and were given bandages. These were applied to his wounds and Dollfuss regained consciousness. Hudl now told him that he would have been spared had he not resisted. Dollfuss replied feebly that he, too, had once been a soldier. This could possibly confirm Planetta's statement that he had tried to strike his attacker. Then Dollfuss asked: "How are my ministers?" The policemen told him they were all right. He murmured: "A major, a captain and several soldiers came in and shot at me." He clearly believed that the intruders were regular army men.

There are several reports, somewhat at variance, about the conversations the dying man held with his captors. According to the SS man Stiastny, a political discussion of sorts went on between the victim and his murderers. One of the rebels blamed him for bringing misery and distress upon the Austrian National Socialists. Dollfuss replied: "I have always tried to do the best I could. I always wanted peace." In that case, another insurgent shouted, Dollfuss should have made peace with Germany. The wounded man stared at the pitiless faces around him, then replied: "Children, you simply don't understand." Later he asked for Schuschnigg. Hudl came into the room again and told him that Schuschnigg was not present. He urged him to order Rintelen to form a new government and stop the armed forces from any action against the chancellery. But to this Dollfuss made no reply. Repeatedly he asked for a physician, but was again refused. He bade the policemen to move his arms and legs, and said, "I feel nothing. I think I am paralyzed." He then asked for a priest. This too was refused.

Nearly all the rebels declared later that their final instructions at the Siebensterngasse gymnasium were to avoid unnecessary bloodshed. They should use their weapons only in an emergency and even then only fire at the legs of those who offered armed resistance. This statement may well be true, as no further shooting occurred. Of course, there had been no resistance, though some of the officials carried pistols. But even the great Major Fey had not resisted capture. Nor did any of the trapped Heimwehr officers and policemen try to fight their way out. It seems that on that day nobody wanted to be a hero.

In the meantime, a number of decisive events had occurred outside the chancellery. At 1 P.M. one group of rebels had captured the Ravag Building almost at the moment the other group had entered the Ballhausplatz. They had broadcast the prearranged announcement that Dollfuss had resigned and that Rintelen was to be the new head of government. But from that moment on, things took a turn that was unexpected. Hardly fifteen minutes after the capture of the chancellery, the building was completely surrounded by Zehner's troops, police detachments, and Fey's Heimwehr regiment, which had come from its Prater training grounds. The first result of that belated action was that the insurgents were now separated from their own leaders. Fridolin Glass wandered around in disguise and was finally arrested again by the police. Waechter, the real brain of the conspiracy, sat in a restaurant near the Ballhausplatz. He had planned to enter the occupied building and conduct negotiations with the captured ministers. He was not aware of the fact that eight of the eleven ministers had long since left the chancellery. And now there was a cordon of troops sealing off the square. Weydenhammer and Rintelen were at the Hotel Imperial.

In truth, the putsch had failed at the moment the eight ministers had left the chancellery. This, and the fact that the

Nazis, as we shall see, did not succeed in capturing President Miklas, decided the failure of the coup d'état before it had begun in earnest. With the President and most members of the Cabinet at liberty, the chance for success had practically evaporated. In consequence, General Zehner kept control of the army and the few Nazis in higher command posts refrained from action. During the rest of that fateful afternoon Vienna remained quiet; no demonstrations or uprisings of any kind took place. The main force of the insurgents was almost immediately surrounded by government forces and thereby neutralized. When the population of the capital became aware of the situation, it remained calm and watched the drama with some detachment. The real revolt took place in the provinces, but it came far too late to have any practical results.

Before we return to Dollfuss lying on his couch, dying in utmost physical and spiritual distress, let us examine more closely the question of planned or accidental murder. Though Planetta did not speak the full truth at his trial, this does not conclusively prove that he committed a calculated crime. It is conceivable that he was just trigger-happy.

However, there are also strong arguments for a completely different conclusion. For a long time assassination of the Chancellor had been widely discussed in National Socialist circles. The Austrian military attaché in Paris, Colonel Lothar Rendulic, later a prominent general in the German army, declared six months before the deed was done that Dollfuss would lose his life and that a National Socialist victory in Austria was a certainty. Far more conclusive is the fact that the instructions to the Austrian Nazis for "Operation Price Shooting" definitely counted on the death of Dollfuss. These orders fell into the hands of the Austrian government on the day after the uprising. A German courier was apprehended by the border police in Kollerschlag, Upper Austria. Hidden in his shirt and in his shoes was a complete list of instructions for the uprising. These papers were later published by the government and became known as the "Kollerschlag Documents." They contained a list of code signals by which the insurgents were to communicate with their friends in Germany. First on that list was a special contingency signal for announcing Dollfuss's death. The code words for that occasion were: "Old cutlery samples arrived."

Admittedly, this is not definite proof that a murder was planned in full detail, but it certainly indicates the atmosphere of the whole enterprise. We have no evidence that Planetta received a firm order for assassination. But one of his superiors may very well have told him that liquidation of Dollfuss was highly desirable. For a fanatical Nazi like Planetta, such a hint would have been sufficient. Many a political murder has been committed without a formal order. Veiled encouragement by proper authority has often guided the hand of an assassin. History is full of examples of such assassinations from Thomas à Becket to Darlan. Perhaps Habicht had hinted to his lieutenants that the Fuehrer would be pleased to see his enemy disappear forever. If one of them passed this information on to Planetta, no further explanations were needed.

No written proof has ever come to light that Hitler or any of his closer associates ordered the assassination. Of course, this means little, because such orders were never put into writing. During the Nazi era enemies of the regime frequently disappeared in a mysterious way, were killed in accidents, or were shot while attempting to escape. The Nazis always stuck to Planetta's story that the killing was a regrettable accident.

If that were true, it is hard to understand why they did not allow a doctor into the building. As we shall see, a great number of phone calls were made from the chancellery on that afternoon. But none went to a physician or a hospital. Planetta's intention to kill might be questionable. The attitude of the rebels toward the wounded Chancellor leaves no doubt.

11

Death in the Chancellery

L ET US LEAVE THEY DYING CHANCELLOR and the besieged building for the present and turn our attention to President
Wilhelm Miklas, whom the Nazis had wanted to capture at
his summer resort on the Woerthersee. This unassuming
man, a former school principal and father of eleven children,
was not highly appreciated by his contemporaries. The
prerogatives of the nominal head of state were modest and
Dr. Miklas was neither a great orator nor a very forceful per-
sonality.

Nevertheless, he was one of the few statesmen of the Austrian republic who lived through this stormy period with clean
hands and an unblemished record of quiet courage. He was
to show his mettle once more in 1938, when his country was
overrun by Germany. Miklas was one of the few, the very few,
who at that tragic moment behaved with decency, character,

and decorum. When pressured by Berlin to appoint as Chancellor a man tainted with treason, he refused with the words: "Austria alone determines who is to be the head of its government." Abandoned by his friends at home and abroad, he finally had to resign, but maintained his dignity to the last. He survived the war and Hitler's defeat to see Austria's resurrection as an independent state. Among a crowd of weaklings, opportunists, and outright traitors he strikes us as a man of integrity.

The Nazi decision to eliminate Miklas simultaneously with their putsch in Vienna was quite logical. Miklas had only hesitatingly approved of Dollfuss's dictatorial regime and would certainly not compromise with a National Socialist junta, risen by violence and sedition. But the small task force sent to capture the President was hastily assembled and failed completely. It was an improvised effort, poorly executed.

The leader of the squad, Max Grillmayer, only arrived from Berlin on July 21, and probably had too little time to prepare his difficult venture carefully. He was well known to the police, as he had taken part in a teargas attack on a department store and the rather pointless murder of a Jewish jeweler. It seems that the police were tipped off about the expedition to Velden. The authorities did not yet realize that a kidnapping of the President was intended and suspected only some illegal action. When the squad arrived in Klagenfurt, it was stopped, and two of the conspirators were arrested. A third, Dr. Ott, brother of one of the two captives, rather stupidly ran into the police trap. Grillmayer and a fifth member of the squad took alarm and fled over the Yugoslav border, which is a mere thirteen miles from Klagenfurt. Only after a thorough examination of the event did it come to light that Grillmayer and the Ott brothers had planned to take the President of Austria into their custody. The two brothers confessed and were later sentenced to long prison terms.

When they were informed of the uprising the eight members of the Cabinet in Vienna convened at the Ministry of Defense, a large ornate building on the Stubenring. Since the Vice Chancellor, Prince Starhemberg, was still vacationing on the Lido, the Minister of Education, Dr. Kurt von Schuschnigg, was elected temporary chairman. His first act was to call Miklas in Velden. The President had been enjoying the day on the lake, totally unaware that a plot against himself had just been foiled. The facts about this affair did not become known until later. After learning of the raid on the chancellery, Miklas acted promptly and decisively. In the first place, Schuschnigg was sworn in over the telephone as provisional Chancellor of Austria. Miklas then ordered him to take immediate action against the rebels. "Use all forces of the government to restore law and order, take measures against the rebels, and, above all, liberate the captive members of the government; they are to be delivered safe and sound from their captivity." These were Miklas's words to the new Chancellor, who found himself suddenly and unexpectedly in an undreamed-of position of power. Fortunately, he had full control of the armed forces, as General Zehner and his staff were now at hand. The problem was how to use them in the most effective manner.

It is understandable that Schuschnigg hesitated to order an immediate attack on the chancellery. The 154 rebels were now completely surrounded and outgunned by a far superior force. But it was feared that an attack would lead to the immediate slaughter of the captive ministers and officials. At that time the Cabinet did not yet know that Dollfuss was slowly dying on his couch. It was decided to negotiate with the insurgents before taking any drastic action. We may well wonder how Dollfuss and Fey would have acted had they been at liberty and some of their colleagues the captives. Would they again have used the guns of February? Schuschnigg's cautious approach undoubtedly saved many lives, but the negotiations with the rebel force and the strange end of the whole affair are far from edifying.

During the morning and early afternoon the government had continually acted with a marked lack of determination. Miklas's order to Schuschnigg was the turning point, though it still took several hours to liquidate the uprising. Meanwhile, general confusion and indecision seemed to infect the rebels. After their initial success, their energy drained from them as if by magic.

The trouble was that the insurgents on the Ballhausplatz were without real leadership. Holzweber—now calling himself "Captain Friedrich"—was a former sergeant able to conduct a coup de main, but no more. The events had overwhelmed him. He later declared at his own trial: "I had been told that there would be no bloodshed, that a new government had already been formed, and that Rintelen was present at the Ballhausplatz. Then, at the chancellery, I missed the leaders of the uprising." Indeed, Holzweber's superior, Fridolin Glass, was still aimlessly wandering about, heavily perspiring in his newly purchased overcoat. The police finally caught him at 3:30 P.M.[1] Holzweber tried in vain to reach Waechter and Weydenhammer at a café where they had congregated several hours before. Waechter himself could not get through the cordon the police had drawn around the chancellery. He tried to contact Dr. Steinhaeusl,

---

1. Glass carried false papers and, strangely enough, the police could not identify him as the leader of SS Standarte 89. After being held under arrest for only eight days, he was released and promptly fled to Germany.

the rebels' collaborator within the police force, but it was now too late to persuade him to act decisively. Weydenhammer claimed later that he managed to slip through the police cordon and tried to gain admission into the building by shouting the prearranged password "Eighty Nine," but the doors remained barred and he was refused admission. This story makes very little sense and was perhaps invented by Weydenhammer as an alibi. He may have feared being accused of cowardice or indecision.

Inside the beleaguered building, the insurgents were getting nervous. They walked aimlessly through the large edifice with its many empty offices. All windows had been closed and the blinds drawn. The hot July sun burned down and the occupying force and their prisoners were perspiring. Commander Holzweber looked out at the Ballhausplatz, which now resembled an armed camp. Finally, he decided to talk to his most prominent captives. He first tried to approach Karwinsky, but the unfortunate Secretary of Security rudely refused to have anything to do with him. Then Holzweber turned to Fey, who seemed more amenable. So far the ministers had been kept under close guard in the Hall of Pillars, but now Fey was marched into the corner room and allowed to speak to Dollfuss. The reports on that last conversation between the two men are somewhat confused. It seems that the dying man impressed on his minister that Mussolini should look after his wife and children. Then he asked about the other members of the Cabinet and said that Schuschnigg should become his successor, as indeed he did. It is characteristic that both Miklas and Dollfuss picked that serious young intellectual. Prince Starhemberg, the Vice Chancellor, was not even considered for the post.

The insurgents, who were surrounding Dollfuss and Fey, were getting impatient. One of them, pistol in hand, shouted:

"Get down to brass tacks, Chancellor, we're not interested in talk. Order Fey to stop the armed forces from any action, and Rintelen should be empowered to form a new government." Dollfuss's reply was vague: "There should be no bloodshed. Rintelen should make peace," he murmured. Of course, he knew nothing about the true situation. He could not know that Schuschnigg's government at the Ministry of Defense was getting ready to function. One insurgent leaned over Dollfuss and cried: "Say what you still have to tell us!" But Dollfuss was already too far gone to reply. His suffering was slowly drawing to its end. He seems to have lost consciousness from time to time; he also complained of feeling suffocated. There was blood on his lips. The two policemen tried to comfort him and wiped his brow. The insurgents still refused to call a doctor or even a priest, though their telephone connection was functioning. There would have been no difficulty in calling in a physician. One of the SS men later maintained that a doctor with an ambulance did actually offer his services twice and was rudely refused entrance. When he appeared a second time, the guards told him that it was now too late for his services. It is not clear how that doctor could have known that anybody within the building was injured. However, as this story originated with one of the insurgents, it may very well be true. The SS man had no earthly reason to invent an episode which showed his comrades as the brutes they certainly were. The cruel and inhuman behavior of the Chancellor's captors was disgusting, whatever Dollfuss's faults. They knew full well that the dying man was a practicing Catholic, and the presence of a priest could not have upset their plans. It is questionable whether a doctor could have saved Dollfuss's life, but Holzweber, Planetta, and the others were in no way qualified to give a medical opinion. The inescapable conclusion is that they wanted Dollfuss to die and that they brutally refused even to mitigate his suffering. It is this attitude that must lead to the verdict that Dollfuss's shooting was willful assassination. And it is their deliberate, coldblooded behavior which makes Holzweber's and Planetta's sentencing an act of justice.

Dollfuss spoke once more to the policemen before he died: "Children, you are so good to me. Why are the others not like you? I only wanted peace. We never attacked, we only had to defend ourselves. May the Lord forgive them. Give my regards to my wife and my children." He spoke no more. He must have died shortly before 4 P.M. For about an hour his death was kept secret. But by 5 P.M. rumors reached the outside that the little Chancellor was dead. It has never been explained who passed the report to the forces on the Ballhausplatz. Perhaps one of the Nazis shouted the news to the soldiers as an act of derision.

Dollfuss must have died in despair, fearing that his government had collapsed and that Austria had already fallen into the hands of the Nazis. In fact, his calm decision to let his Cabinet disperse before it was too late gave his country a respite of four years. Its final fall in March 1938 was due more to foreign developments than to internal causes.

The rebels now decided to use Emil Fey as an intermediate. And here, indeed, they found a willing collaborator. During the next hours Fey played an extremely peculiar and far from honorable part in the liquidation of the putsch. His actions within those hours would destroy his political career and eventually would cost him his life, though that reckoning was still four years away.

We have already mentioned that Fey had been resentful of his diminished power within the Dollfuss government. It is at least probable that Fey maintained secret contacts with the National Socialists through one of his aides, a certain Major

Lahr. There is no definite proof that Fey intended to overthrow the government. The Nazi documents that fell into
Austrian hands clearly referred to him as an enemy. Nevertheless, there was in Fey a tendency, a willingness to collaborate
with almost anybody who would offer him an influential job.
The SS man Fritz Lehrer later told the Germans that he over-
heard a conversation between Fey and Holzweber which took
place in the telephone exchange of the chancellery. According to Lehrer, Holzweber offered Fey the post of Minister of
Security—his previous Department!—in Rintelen's Cabinet.
Fey hestitated and asked exactly what powers he would control in that office. Holzweber replied that not only all police
forces but also the SA and SS would be under Fey's command.
To this proposal Fey is supposed to have replied: "Very well,
then I accept."

This incident is somewhat doubtful, because Holzweber
had no authority to offer ministerial appointments to anyone.
Even had the putsch succeeded, there is no reason to assume
that Dr. Rintelen as Austrian Chancellor would have honored
the promises of a mere SS officer, commanding a band of
cutthroats. As to Fey, could he have been so naïve as to take
such a promise seriously? Or did he only try to lead his captors on to gain time?

Lehrer also claims that Fey telephoned the president of
police, Dr. Seydel, and informed him that he, Fey, was the new
Minister of Security. In any case, Fey wrote a proclamation,
directed to the people of Austria and to the armed forces, in
which he stated that:

1. Dr. Dollfuss had been injured and resigned from the
government.

2. He had appointed Dr. Rintelen as his successor.

3. All armed forces were now under Fey's command.

This pencil-written piece of paper was handed to the policeman Kamba, who was permanently stationed in the chancellery and was a rebel sympathizer. Kamba was allowed to leave the building and he forwarded the message to Dr. Seydel, whose office was only a few blocks away. It seems that Kamba also wished to contact Rintelen, but Seydel immediately hastened to the Ministry of Defense, taking Kamba along. In the end this peculiar proclamation only compromised Rintelen, who was arrested shortly afterward. In the meantime, Fey made several more attempts to act as a contact man between the insurgents and the legal government.

Obviously, the rebels felt that time was running out and that only desperate measures could save the day. "Major" Hudl walked down into the courtyard and read a proclamation to his assembled prisoners, who were told that Rintelen was now the head of a new "national government." A few hands went up and some shouted "Heil Hitler!" but the majority remained silent.

Upstairs, the French windows above the main entrance were opened and Fey, Holzweber, and a few others appeared on a semicircular balcony. One of the rebels held a pistol to Fey's back, another had his hands around Fey's ankles to prevent him from jumping down. The Heimwehr men on the square greeted their leader with encouraging shouts and threatened to hang the Nazis from the lampposts if Fey were hurt. The major tried to calm them down: "Comrades, the persons within the chancellery are in danger, but everything will be all right!" Then he called for the senior police officer to advance and walk to a rear entrance of the building. Upon reaching the door, this officer was admitted and confronted by Fey and the rebel leaders. He was told that Dollfuss was wounded and had requested that there be no more violence. Fey added that the President had ordered Rintelen to act as a mediator. Therefore, no action should be undertaken by the armed forces. They must wait until Rintelen appeared on the scene and issued further orders.

With that message, the astonished police officer was again pushed out of the building. While he hastened to inform the government, Fey made several phone calls to the broadcasting station, the police, and lastly to the Ministry of Defense. There he got his colleague Neustaedter-Stuermer on the wire and learned that Schuschnigg had formed a new government and was in no mood to surrender to the rebels. From this moment on the Nazis must have realized that their game was up. Both the President and the new government were at liberty; nothing had been heard of Rintelen, and the hoped-for revolt of the army had never taken place. Schuschnigg was in full control of all government forces and the attack on the Ravag Building had also failed. The insurgents merely controlled the chancellery and held two ministers and a number of civil servants as hostages.

The telephone conversation between Fey and Neustaedter-Stuermer seems to have taken place at 4:35 P.M. When asked about Dollfuss's injuries, Fey told his colleague: "They are rather serious." By that time Dollfuss was already dead.

The Austrian government published a report on the revolt which appeared several weeks after the event. Most of it is factual; no attempt was made to deny or omit the mistakes made by the police. However, Fey's part—especially the role he played after Dollfuss had been shot—was minimized, and in that respect the document was a whitewash. The man who edited the report admitted later that he had omitted details incriminating Fey. This was confirmed by Starhemberg in his memoirs, and by Schuschnigg in his last book, in which he described his struggle against Hitler. Both men had no liking for Fey, but they feared that the full truth would undermine confidence in their shaky government. Besides, the Vienna

Heimwehr regiments were extremely loyal to the major, and the prompt removal of their hero might have led to mutiny. Therefore it was decided to treat Fey gently and keep him in the government, at least temporarily. However, his strange behavior had come to the notice of too many persons. The result was the most fantastic rumors. It was even whispered that not Planetta, but Fey had murdered Dollfuss. This is utter nonsense; but many people sensed that Fey had not behaved as an officer and a gentleman.

12

Attack and Counterattack

WHILE THE MAIN FORCE OF THE SS STANDARTE 89 struck the chancellery, a smaller squad went into action against the building of the Austrian Broadcasting Company at the Johannesgasse. The attack had been well planned and the insurgents were informed about conditions within the building. However, they did not know that there was a second communication switchboard and broadcasting station in an adjacent building. Because of a previous attempt at sabotage, the main building was guarded by a police inspector and a member of the auxiliary police force. At 12:30 P.M., two more policemen arrived and informed the inspector that they had been ordered to assist him. They were told to guard the entrance.

Meanwhile the SS squad had assembled at a café and then split into two groups which approached the building separately from different directions. Altogether the attacking force consisted merely of fifteen men, all of them inconspicuous civilians. At 1 P.M., one of them walked up to the entrance and said he had an appointment with an executive of the broadcasting company. As he was being admitted, his companions quickly overpowered the auxiliary policeman. The two newly arrived guards, who were part of the plot, surrendered without resistance. The police inspector, who had posted himself at the other side of the street, came running and was immediately shot to death by the intruders. They could now safely enter the building and barricade the entrance.

At the same time the second group of insurgents occupied an adjoining school building. That school had a courtyard which bordered on the radio station; the Nazis easily climbed through the windows on the ground floor. After they shot two more guards, they drove the employees into one room and forced the radio announcer to read the following message: "The Dollfuss government has resigned. Dr. Rintelen has taken control of the government." The telephone room was occupied at the same time and the operator was forced to cut all communications.

Since the Nazis were ignorant of the second switchboard, it continued functioning, and the imprisoned manager called for help and ordered the broadcasting station disconnected from the big Bisamberg radio transmitter. Within minutes the radio building was surrounded by police. As the main entrance was now barricaded, the attack had to be made through other buildings, over the roofs and a small backyard which was exposed to the fire of the SS. Another policeman was killed, but the intruders were now besieged. The radio continued to send out popular music without making any further announcements. Ironically, several persons called up Dr. Rintelen to congratulate him.

To the Nazis in the province, that radio message was the long-awaited signal for revolt and it was obeyed, though with considerable delay. But the capital remained strangely quiet, except for the Johannesgasse, where a bitter battle was now going on between the police and the SS. It took the police an hour and forty-five minutes and several hand grenades to force the Nazis to surrender. In the end, thirteen of them were driven to the top floor and captured. One had been killed and another managed to escape in the general confusion. The two policemen who had made the invasion possible quickly gave up when their colleagues outside began throwing hand grenades. One more man, a radio actor, who had lost his nerve during the gun battle and tried to run from the building, was killed accidentally.

The failure of the Ravag seizure had decisive consequences. It meant that the rebels were now without a voice and that their man of straw, Dr. Anton Rintelen, was exposed without being able to take any action. As for the insurgents outside Vienna, they had been called to arms at the wrong moment. Of course, not everybody had heard the Austrian radio at 1 P.M., and many hours passed before the word got around. When "Operation Price Shooting" finally got underway, the Vienna putsch had already failed. Particularly in Carinthia, where the Nazis were quite strong, the revolt only got started on July 26. At that time, the government had the situation well in hand. As a crowning irony, Adolf Hitler had by then washed his hands of the whole affair and was "sharply condemning the attack on the Austrian Chancellor." No greater hypocrisy had been uttered since Queen Elizabeth I of England shrilly denounced the execution of Mary, Queen of Scots, which she herself had ordered.

Rintelen himself was still sitting quietly in his hotel room when Waechter and Weydenhammer, by now generals without an army, came rushing in, imploring him to take immediate action. But Rintelen, who had already been seriously disturbed on the eve of the events, realized that things were in a very bad way. It was now four o'clock and nothing indicated that the day could still be saved for the insurgents. Within three hours the situation had changed materially. For Rintelen now to assume leadership of a gang of rebels who had disguised themselves as soldiers was simply unthinkable. That was not at all the way the great intriguer had planned his accession to the Ballhausplatz. He would have been only too happy to sever quickly every connection with that mob and its leaders, but it was now too late. With the legal government sitting at the Department of Defense building and the Federal President unexpectedly free and safe at Velden, Rintelen had no desire to get further involved. We may wonder if the thought of having his two inconvenient guests arrested passed through his mind.

While the three conspirators were still arguing, the telephone rang and a messenger from Dr. Schuschnigg's government was announced by the hotel manager downstairs. Waechter and Weydenhammer hastily slipped behind a curtain and in walked Dr. Friedrich Funder, editor-in-chief of the Catholic newspaper *Reichspost,* an old adversary of Rintelen's. Funder earnestly told Rintelen that his prompt appearance was urgently demanded by the government. After some hesitation, Rintelen followed Funder out of the hotel lobby. Outside Funder and a second man, a muscular fellow named Edgar Tibor Rados, grabbed him and pulled him into a car. They drove him to the Ministry of Defense, only a few minutes from the Hotel Imperial. At the ministry, Rintelen was confined to a room, and when an official came to tell him that two gentlemen were waiting for him, he realized that this meant arrest. He pulled out a gun and made a clumsy attempt to shoot himself, putting a bullet into his left side. On his table two letters to relatives were found in which he claimed that his name had been misused and that consequently he was putting an end to his life. However, the bullet wound was not fatal. He was brought to a hospital and was off the critical list within a few days. The government reluctantly proceeded to put him on trial for high treason. There had been too much publicity about the case to hush it up.

The two Nazi leaders slipped out of the Hotel Imperial unaware of Rintelen's predicament. They tried in vain to reach him at the Department of Defense. Thereupon they attempted to contact their friends in the Austrian army, but those gentlemen were none too eager to continue the relationship. With General Zehner in firm command, any belated action by subordinate officers would certainly have ended in disaster. They shrugged, declaring that they had been left without information regarding the progress of the revolt. Therefore they had remained inactive. Very likely Sinzinger and his colleagues never had any intention of exposing themselves. They would have shown their hand had the putsch succeeded. There is no indication that they were even inclined to stick their necks out during the initial phase. Their attitude has a fatal similarity to the inactivity of so many German anti-Nazi officers in July 1944, when an attempt was made to overthrow Hitler.

Waechter now tried to stir the dormant mass of Viennese Nazis into action. He figured that "Operation Price Shooting" was now well underway in the provinces. Vienna could still join the developing civil war. True, his own opinion about the SA had never been very high—but in this critical situation one had to try everything. Waechter had never been on good terms with the SA leadership, and the role of this organization in the coup d'état had not been clearly determined. In fact,

Habicht had ordered him to leave the SA alone. There is even reason to assume that certain elements in the SA were actively working against the SS. Waechter later accused the SA leadership of treason, claiming that the whole organization was riddled with informers.

However, on that frantic afternoon, Waechter made an attempt to save his faltering revolt by appealing to SA leaders. He hurriedly met with an SA leader called Tuerk and a few others, and was promised immediate help. The SA was supposed to march to the Ballhausplatz and liberate the surrounded SS Standarte 89. Such, at any rate, was the story told later by Waechter and Weydenhammer in their separate reports. If it is true, they had reasons for their complaints, because nothing happened. Not a single SA man was ever seen near the chancellery. Tuerk and his men probably realized that their loosely organized, ill-armed supporters were no match for the Austrian army. Perhaps they were not too unhappy to see Waechter fail. It must be remembered that Hitler had executed a number of SA leaders only four weeks before with the aid of the SS.

Waechter then made a desperate effort to come to an agreement with the Heimwehr. This seems absolutely fantastic, as at this very moment Nazis and Heimwehr were on the eve of a bloody battle in the provinces. Within the next few days the two factions were to fight each other with the greatest ferocity. Waechter's report about his negotiations with one of Fey's men, Captain Kuglmayer, must be taken with reserve. On the other hand, Fey's strange behavior during the whole afternoon makes one suspect that this story is at least not pure invention. According to Waechter, Kuglmayer declared that Fey had informed him by phone from the chancellery that such cooperation was possible. Allegedly, Fey was willing to discuss common action and order his men, temporarily under

Dollfuss in his uniform as a first lieutenant.

Austrian troops in action during the civil war in February 1934.

Dollfuss with army officers at the bridgehead on the Danube during the civil war in February 1934.

Dollfuss greeting General Schoenburg-Hartenstein and his men after the February revolt.

The Heimwehr leaders Prince Starhemberg and Major Emil Fey.

Franz Holzweber,
the leader of the
SS raid on the
chancellery.

Otto Planetta, the
man who shot
Dollfuss.

Dr. Anton Rintelen.

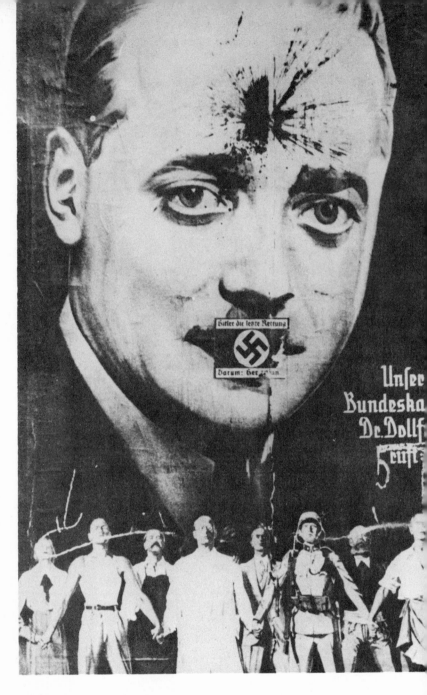

Dollfuss poster defaced with swastika.

120

The battle for the Ravag Building on July 25, 1934. A dead policeman is carried off.

In front of the Ravag Building. A fallen guard is removed by the
coridon.

The chancellery, encircled by police troops, after its occupation by the Nazis.

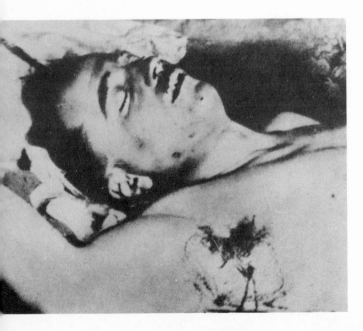

Dollfuss, lying dead on his couch in the chancellery.

President Miklas and the new Chancellor Schuschnigg at Dollfuss's funeral.

Four years later. The Nazis dedicating a plaque in memory of the July revolt at the chancellery.

OPPOSITE: Memorial to Dollfuss at the Church of the Dormition in Jerusalem.

AUSTRIA MARIAE ASSUMPTAE

the command of one of his deputies, not to fire on the rebel forces. Fey's colleague and rival in command of the Heimwehr, the Vice Chancellor Prince Starhemberg, was to be arrested at the airport on his return from Italy.

It is very difficult to decide the authenticity of this story, which became known only in 1964, fully thirty years after the event. If Fey was willing at that late hour to make common cause with the Nazis and even have one member of the legal government arrested, he can only be judged as a traitor to his country. There is no proof of this charge aside from the aforementioned reports, admittedly written by men who mainly tried to justify their own failure. On the other hand, it is not easy to understand why Weydenhammer and Waechter should invent this episode, which discredited Fey but bestowed no great merit on themselves. By the time these alleged contacts took place, the cause of the rebels was already lost. After the new Austrian Cabinet had deliberated almost three hours without taking decisive action, Schuschnigg finally made up his mind to issue an ultimatum to the rebels. It read: "If there is no loss of life on the side of the members of the government who have been unlawfully held prisoners, then the Cabinet grants the rebels safe conduct and passage across the border. If the deadline for surrender is not obeyed, the full force of the government will be used." General Zehner and Minister Neustaedter-Stuermer were delegated to the chancellery to order the rebels out of the building within fifteen minutes.

Schuschnigg always maintained that when he dictated that ultimatum he was unaware of Dollfuss's death. This is probably true. The first messenger, Franz Kamba, had only said that Dollfuss was wounded. Fey's phone conversation with Neustaedter-Stuermer, in which the Chancellor's injuries were described as "rather serious," took place at about 4:35 P.M.

Shortly afterward, the two ministers drove to the Ballhaus-platz. At that time rumors about Dollfuss's death were already spreading, but the fact was not definitely confirmed until 6 P.M. That timing is important because the Nazis later claimed that the government had been well aware that Dollfuss was dead when the ultimatum was issued.

At his Adriatic resort, Starhemberg was also ignorant of Dollfuss's fate. It was the Italian government, not Vienna, that informed him of the seriousness of the situation. An Italian plane was put at his disposal. However, the plane ran into very bad weather over the Alps and Starhemberg was forced to return to Venice. It was only on the following morning, when everything was over, that he was able to reach Vienna. In the meantime, he had alerted his Heimwehr troops from Italy by telephone and this contributed to the speedy defeat of the Nazi uprising in the provinces.

At 5:30 P.M., a ludicrous scene took place in front of the chancellery. Fey and the rebel leaders had again appeared on the balcony, while Neustaedter-Stuermer, ultimatum in hand, stood below amidst the crowd of soldiers, police troops, and Heimwehr men. Fey asked: "Where is Rintelen?" Neustaedter-Stuermer replied laconically: "He is not coming." Rintelen was by now under confinement. The minister read the ultimatum while a great silence fell over the square. He ended: "If you don't surrender within twenty minutes, I will have the troops storm the building." Fey shouted back: "I forbid any attack!" Neustaedter-Stuermer was not to be moved: "You have nothing to forbid. You are a prisoner. It is now five thirty-five P.M. At five fifty-five we shall attack." The rebels and Fey disappeared from the balcony and General Zehner started getting his men ready. But then action was delayed again. Fey wanted another parley. This time it was conducted through a barred window at street level. The rebels, understandably fearing for their lives, wanted a detailed agreement about the terms of surrender. The not very dignified wrangling went on for more than an hour. Finally, on Neustaedter-Stuermer's "word of honor as an officer" it was agreed that the insurgents should lay down their arms. Then, without further investigation, they should be allowed to board trucks and be driven to the German border. During these prolonged talks the military might of the government—several thousand men strong—stood impassively on the square, doing absolutely nothing.

The Nazis claimed later that Neustaedter-Stuermer's word of honor was a deliberate deception. He himself declared that he knew nothing of Dollfuss's death when he delivered the ultimatum. He was not believed and the episode sealed his fate in 1938, when the SS got its chance to revenge itself on former adversaries. Neustaedter-Stuermer became one of the first victims of the *Anschluss.*

The insurgents inside the besieged chancellery, fully realizing that their coup de'état had failed, were now bargaining for their lives. Their hope that Fey would come over to their side, or at least intercede for them, was also fading rapidly. Holzweber had his doubts about any promises once his force had laid down its weapons. In desperation he decided to ask for intervention from the side he had been fighting for: the German Reich, represented by its ambassador in Vienna.

13

Safe Conduct

D R. KURT RIETH, GERMAN AMBASSADOR IN VIENNA , was a leftover from the old regime. He was a diplomat of the Weimar Republic who—like so many others—had been taken over by Hitler. He had always shown misgivings about the new German policy toward Austria. That is not to say that Rieth objected to the idea of the *Anschluss,* but he was perturbed by the mounting Nazi terror. Repeatedly he had warned the Wilhelmstrasse that the Austrian Nazis were getting out of hand and would finally land the Reich in a mess of international dimensions. It can be said with certainty that Rieth knew nothing about the preparations for the coup d'état, though at least one of his subordinates, Guenther von Altenburg, certainly did. Rieth was under orders from the Wilhelmstrasse not to get involved with Austrian Nazis.

During the late afternoon of July 25, the telephone rang at

the German embassy and a man who introduced himself as "Captain Friedrich, leader of the rebels," announced that he wished to talk to the ambassador. So far, Rieth had only heard that an attack on the chancellery had taken place and that Dollfuss had been wounded. He had sent this piece of news on to the Foreign Ministry in Berlin at 5 P.M. Holzweber, using his *nom de guerre* Friedrich, informed the ambassador that the putsch had failed and asked for his intervention. The rebels were to be given safe conduct to the German frontier and the ambassador was asked to be personal witness to the agreement between them and the Austrian government. Had Rieth been a very intelligent man, he would most certainly have refused to intercede in an affair of such peculiar nature. Indeed, he hesitated; but immediately afterward he was again called by Fey, who offered further explanations and urged Rieth to hasten to the Ballhausplatz. While Fey was making his phone call, Holzweber stood next to him. At that time Fey was only too eager to get the whole matter finally settled and regain his freedom. Rieth eventually agreed to come but emphasized that he was doing so only in a private, not an official capacity.

His telephone communication with Berlin had been cut off during the later part of the afternoon and there was no way for him to contact any superior authority. Weydenhammer, if he is to be believed, must have been almost omnipresent that afternoon, for he claimed he had warned the ambassador against any involvement. There is no proof of that as for so many other of his statements. Weydenhammer had no contact with Holzweber, who was in the chancellery during the critical hours, and it is hard to understand how he could have foretold the rebels' appeal to the German embassy. But even if he had issued such a warning, it had no effect. Without considering the consequences, the Reich's ambassador hastened to deal with persons who were clearly in revolt against the legal government.

When Rieth arrived at the Ballhausplatz, bargaining about the terms of the safe conduct was still in progress. The rebels wanted a military escort, and Neustaedter-Stuermer was willing to grant it. He must have been astonished and irritated by Rieth's sudden appearance. The situation was indeed unique. Here was a Cabinet minister parleying with rebels who had just killed the head of his government and who held several hundred persons as hostages. And now, to top it all, the envoy of a foreign power turned up to act as a sort of referee. Rieth announced that he was appearing only because he had been requested to and insisted that he was present as a private party. Of course, this was sheer nonsense. The rebels wanted him as Hitler's representative, being under the illusion that their idol would grant them protection. Holzweber and his men did not for a moment suspect that they would be sacrificed with the greatest ease once the Fuehrer considered them a liability.

Neustaedter-Stuermer, a blunt man, told Rieth: "What has to be done here is our affair. Your intervention is unnecessary. I cannot recommend that you soil yourself by negotiations with rebels." Rieth replied that under these circumstances he could do nothing, but he stayed nevertheless.

The next to join the discussion was Fey, who had finally been allowed to leave the chancellery. He reported that Dollfuss was dead.[1] Logically, this should have ended any further negotiations, because Schuschnigg's directive granted free passage to the rebels only if no loss of life had occurred. However, neither Fey nor Neustaedter-Stuermer raised the

---

1. Prior to his release Fey had not mentioned that Dollfuss was dead.

point at this moment. A police officer asked Rieth to speak to Erwin Karwinsky, the State Secretary of Security, who was still being held in the building. Rieth—rather foolishly—asked Neustaedter-Stuermer if he had any objections to such a conversation. The latter shrugged, declining to express an opinion. Rieth's dilemma was ended by Karwinsky himself, who had meanwhile seen a chance to sneak out of the chancellery. The rebels were now too concerned with their own necks to pay much attention. Fey and Karwinsky both insisted that Rieth speak to "Captain Friedrich" and assure him that safe conduct to the border had been granted.

Perhaps Rieth felt that he was already too deeply involved to say no. He allowed the two liberated ministers to guide him to a rear entrance. A door was opened very slightly and the ambassador spoke through that crack to Holzweber standing inside. Rieth declared that everything was settled. The rebels would be conducted to the German border in trucks under an escort of Austrian troops. Then he turned around and, walking to his car, remarked to Karwinsky: "What a crazy affair!" Karwinsky had been a prisoner for six hours and had seen Dollfuss die. He was in no mood to be diplomatic. "I find it peculiar, your Excellency," he replied, "that you have no other expression for that terrible event. The guilt for the blood which was spilled lies across our frontier!"

Rieth made no comment and drove back to his embassy. The telephone connection to Berlin was restored only at 9:45 P.M. At that time he informed the German Foreign Office that the putsch had failed and that Dollfuss was dead and the rebels were on their way to the border under escort. In reality the rebels had become captives because in the meantime another turn of events had occurred.

Schuschnigg had now been informed by an official named Kemptner that Dollfuss was dead. He appeared at the Ballhausplatz when the rebels were on the point of surrender. The army trucks for their transport were ready, the great gate was finally opened, and the insurgents laid down their weapons. At last, the government forces, passive for so long, could occupy the chancellery. Of course, Dollfuss's half naked, blood-spattered body was immediately discovered. Now the moment of reckoning had arrived.

Schuschnigg declared that the terms of his ultimatum had not been fulfilled. He had granted a safe conduct under the condition that no lives were lost. But a murder had occurred. Therefore, the promise of safe conduct was not valid. The rebels were to be arrested and interned under military guard. The Heimwehr came pretty close to shooting them all, right there on the spot, but was restrained. The captive insurgents were allowed to mount trucks, but their trip was very brief. They were imprisoned at the police barracks at the Marokkanergasse. Some were dazed by the sudden turn of events. They had left notes for their families, announcing that they were on their way to Germany.

There has been a great deal of controversy about this procedure. When Schuschnigg formulated this ultimatum he thought that Dollfuss was alive. Possibly Neustaedter-Stuermer was of the same opinion when he read it to the besieged insurgents, though rumors about the Chancellor's death were already circulating. Certainly the truth became known when Fey spoke to Neustaedter-Stuermer after leaving the chancellery. The latter could still have declared that the deal was off. However, he did not refer to Dollfuss at all but calmly waited until the rebels surrendered. It is understandable that they felt betrayed. Of course, the question remains about the validity of an agreement with a group of cutthroats, disguised as soldiers, holding several hundred persons as hostages. Still, Neustaedter-Stuermer had given his word of honor and engaged in long negotiations with them. At best, it was most questionable behavior and the Nazis used it later as propaganda.

Considering the enormous superiority of its forces, the government could easily have taken the building by a concentrated attack. The besiegers had tanks and artillery and an unlimited supply of ammunition. As it turned out later, the insurgents were poorly equipped. They had rifles and pistols but only one machine gun. The truck that carried the heavier arms and most of the ammunition had remained at Siebeusterngasse and was confiscated by the police. However, there was the danger that the rebels would kill their prisoners if an attack occurred, and Schuschnigg was by nature opposed to unnecessary bloodshed. He was to take the same attitude in 1938, when faced with German invasion.

The subject of safe conduct was discussed at a Cabinet meeting the next day, after Starhemberg had finally returned to Vienna. By then Hitler himself had completely disavowed the rebels and condemned the murder of Dollfuss. The Austrian government could now safely take harsh measures against the insurgents, who were abandoned by their local leaders and by the German dictator. A military court, presided over by a civil judge, was appointed to deal with them. It convened for the first time on July 30, with Holzweber and Planetta in the dock.

There was one more casualty, even before the executions began. Johann Dobler, who had so frantically tried to betray the conspiracy, had been captured with the rest. It must be assumed that he would have got off lightly, as he had really made strenuous efforts to forestall the raiders. But seemingly he was overwhelmed by his own guilt feelings. He had betrayed both his government and his friends. While being escorted to an interrogation on July 29, he suddenly broke away from his guards and flung himself from a window into a yard. The full story of his betrayal was published only a few weeks after his death.

Subsequently, the ramifications of the plot came to light and a great number of conspirators and accessories were arrested, among them several high police officers, including Dr. Steinhaeusl, a noted criminologist, who spent the following years in prison.[1] The real ringleaders, Waechter and Weydenhammer, escaped. They had held their last conference while their task force was getting ready to capitulate. True to form, their last council of war was again held in a café, the Viktoria, not far from the chancellery. Pretending they were engaged in a card game, they avoided suspicion. Weydenhammer, with his false British passport, easily made it to Prague. By the following day he was already reporting to his chief, Theo Habicht, on the disaster. A few hours later Habicht was fired by Hitler and disappeared from the political scene.

In Vienna, the uprising had only lasted about six hours, and except for the battle at the Johannesgasse there had been no real fighting. A large part of the Viennese population was actually unaware of what was going on. As it was an ordinary working day, most people were at their normal occupations when it all started. Stores, factories, and offices functioned during the hot, steamy afternoon. Of course, there were all sorts of rumors and wild stories, but even for knowledgeable persons it was hard to form a coherent opinion. After the false broadcast about Dollfuss's resignation, there was a long interval without new announcements. Then followed a report that the government was still in office, but hours *passed* before a more or less accurate news story was published. Most Austri-

---

1. He was released shortly before the *Anschluss* and appointed president of police, but died in 1940.

ans learned of the events only on the second morning from their heavily censored newspapers. The German radio kept announcing Rintelen's chancellorship until late into the night.

The most violent reaction came from Italy. At 4 P.M. Benito Mussolini got the first news from the Schuschnigg government and promptly ordered four Italian army divisions to the Brenner Pass and the Carinthian border. Had German troops intervened in Austria, the Italian army would have crossed the frontier. The possibility of such an event had been envisaged for months. Long before the outbreak of the revolt sufficient troops had been kept south of the border. On the following day, Mussolini firmly declared that he would defend Austria's independence under all circumstances. This was no mere threat. A complete plan (plan "K") for the occupation of southern Austria had been worked out early in the year. Instructions to the Italian forces were based on the possibility of clashes with Austrian rebels as well as with regular German units. Undoubtedly, the Italian army would have marched into Austria had not Schuschnigg's government defeated the insurgents within two days. On July 27, while fighting was still in progress in Carinthia, the Italian infantry, based on Vitipeno—eight miles from the border—was issued battle ammunition. The Germans were fully informed about that situation.

14
Civil War

THE ORIGINAL PLAN TO CAPTURE VIENNA and the Austrian government must be called ingenious. "Operation Price Shooting," the subsequent uprising in the provinces, was poorly organized. Of course, it had no chance of succeeding after "Operation Summer Festival," the Vienna revolt, had failed. It is fruitless to speculate what would have happened had the rebels captured Dollfuss, Miklas, and the whole Cabinet. Most likely this would have led to an invasion by Italian troops.

Aside from these considerations, "Operation Price Shooting" could have succeeded only if launched with lightning speed. The raid on the Ballhausplatz should have been followed by immediate revolt throughout the country. In that case much of Austria could have been in the hands of the rebels before a foreign power could move to intervene. Per-

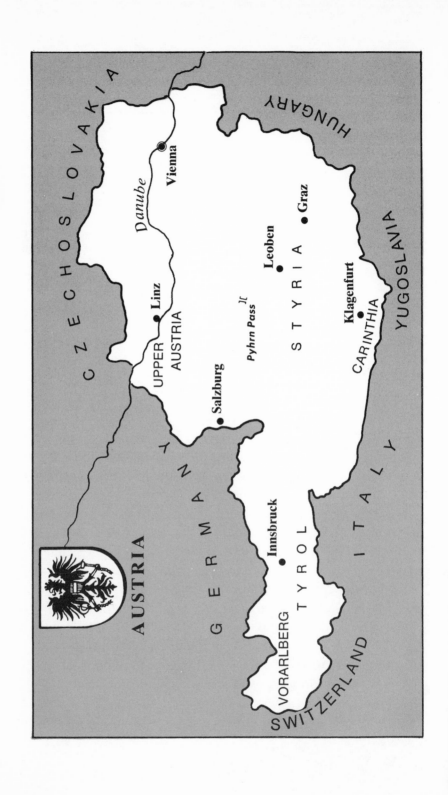

haps the German initiators of the putsch hoped that speedy victory would create a *fait accompli*, which Italy and the West would accept. Hitler's view on that subject is not known. Perhaps he had really been misinformed by Habicht and believed in a bloodless coup d'état and a prompt take-over by Rintelen. It is also possible that he was simply willing to take a calculated risk. The report about Dollfuss's resignation, broadcast at 1 P.M. over the Vienna transmitter, was to be the signal for a general revolt. But organization was haphazard and uneven. In Lower Austria and the Burgenland, the provinces adjoining the capital, only a few minor incidents occurred. Consequently, the eastern part of the country remained firmly in the hands of the government. In Upper Austria, Salzburg, and Tyrol, there were serious disturbances but they were quickly suppressed. In those provinces the Nazis had neither the strength nor the organization to overthrow the local authorities. In Styria and Carinthia, the revolt reached more dangerous proportions. In some smaller towns the insurgents gained temporary successes but were defeated when Austrian army units moved into action.

Two more factors made the revolt a hopeless undertaking. In the first place, it did not start until after the coup d'état in Vienna had already failed. The government was therefore forewarned and could direct its forces to the critical areas. Secondly, the Nazi plan of action fell into government hands on July 26, when a courier was arrested at Kollerschlag, about twenty miles from the border town of Passau. This document proved beyond doubt that the whole uprising had been aided, abetted, and supplied by Germany.

It can also be assumed that the insurgents had hoped for the active assistance of the "Austrian Legion." This unit, about 15,000 men strong, was militarily trained and possessed not only infantry arms but also mortars and artillery.

The Legion had already caused a number of incidents during the preceding weeks, much to the annoyance of the German Minister of Foreign Affairs, Konstantin von Neurath. The Austrian emigrants of the Legion were concentrated along the frontier. Four days before the revolt, a larger unit was posted at Bad Aibling, north of the Austrian border.

The Legion did, in fact, undertake some minor attacks on Austrian territory. On July 27, a group of about fifty men occupied a customs office and advanced to the little town of Kollerschlag, where they were driven back by police. A second attempt had been prepared at Kufstein in the Tyrol, but the legionnaires were disarmed by German police.

In Innsbruck, capital of Tyrol, the revolt began right after the false radio message about Dollfuss's resignation. A police commander, who was known to be very hostile to the Nazis, was ambushed and killed by a member of the SS. This was to be the signal for the uprising, but the local authorities acted immediately and the revolt never really developed. The killer of the police officer was later executed.

In Salzburg, that great center of tourism, the situation remained quiet. Several groups of insurgents were disarmed and arrested before they could undertake any serious action. A somewhat critical situation arose in some small towns, especially at Seekirchen, where the rebels raided the police barracks. A bloody but totally senseless rebel operation was undertaken on the night of July 27, when all possible chances for success were long gone. A group of Nazi insurgents were entrenched in the village of Lamprechtshausen, about twenty miles from Salzburg. The following morning they were attacked by far superior army and Heimwehr forces and quickly captured. The enraged Heimwehr troops treated their captives none too gently. Those who survived were imprisoned in the medieval dungeon of the fortress Hohensalzburg, where conditions were far from hygienic. On many occasions Nazis and Heimwehr fought each other with a savagery heretofore unmatched in Austria.

Upper Austria, too, became the scene of some fighting. The famous resort places of Bad Ischl and Gmunden were disturbed by minor military clashes, but here, too, the rebels were quickly defeated. A far more serious battle took place at the strategic Pyhrn Pass, which connects Upper Austria with Styria. The insurgents occupied that region on July 25. When regular troops reached the top of the mountain pass next day, they were greeted with a hail of bullets from the enemy, who were well entrenched in gorges and quarries. The army suffered considerable losses in that difficult country, but finally artillery was brought into action. The rebels' headquarters were blown up. Alpine troops drove the Nazis back into the forest after bitter fighting.

In Styria, the Nazis were numerically strong and acted quickly when called into action. In the industrial town of Leoben, they succeeded in capturing station houses and various government buildings. The local police could not defeat the well-equipped rebel force which surrounded the town on the morning of July 26. But again, the regular army moved in with artillery and forced the insurgents to surrender.

The Nazis also gained temporary success in the steel center of Donawitz, where they occupied the police barracks and forced the capitulation of a Heimwehr detachment. But again, the army intervened and defeated the rebels, although only after bitter fighting. The Styrian Nazis were comparatively well prepared; in one small town the swastika was raised on the courthouse only thirty minutes after the false radio announcement had come over the air. At Selzthal, the SA occupied the railroad station and blocked a vital tunnel with an armed train. However, they were unsuccessful in Graz, capital of Styria, which had a strong and loyal garrison. An attempt was made to liberate several hundred Nazi prisoners held at an internment camp on the fringe of the city. But the guards had been alerted and the attackers were driven back by machine-gun fire.

With the prompt defeat of the insurgents in Styria, the dangerous rising in Carinthia remained isolated, having started very late. A few bombings during the days before the actual putsch had put the authorities on the alert. The garrison of Klagenfurt, the provincial capital, was strengthened by an additional batallion from Vienna and several known Nazi leaders were arrested. Probably this upset the schedule of the plotters. All remained quiet on July 25. The next morning, the police raided the apartment of a certain Kurt Zechner, who was just then organizing the uprising with some of his comrades. Documents found indicated that the rebellion was to start at noon.

Actually, it began three hours later at the town of Wolfsberg, where the rebels were very well organized and soon overwhelmed the local police. Regular troops were hastily dispatched but were encircled by the insurgents. The commander, Major Smolle, was killed in action. Posters went up, informing the population that the Nazis were taking over the administration. Their reign lasted exactly twenty-four hours, however. By then strong army forces marched on Wolfsberg and the rebels hastily evacuated the town. As the government controlled all rail connections and most major roads, it had no difficulty moving its troops to endangered areas.

The same pattern of action was pursued in Bleiburg, Feldkirchen, and Radenthein. The Nazis achieved some initial success but were unable to hold their positions. They had intended to take Klagenfurt on July 27 by an attack from the Lavant valley, which they controlled until the middle of that day. But then strong army troops with far superior equipment were approaching, and leaflets dropped from planes announced the victory of the government in all other parts of Austria. The insurgents were no match for well-armed troops; they retreated in pouring rain to a prepared position at Rabenstein, close to the Yugoslav border. Lacking food and completely isolated, their situation was now hopeless. On July 30, they abandoned their last stronghold and most of their remaining forces crossed into Yugoslavia. The Austrian troops made no great effort to prevent their flight.

Several small groups also managed to reach Yugoslav territory in that region of lakes and forests. All were disarmed and interned but rather well treated by the Yugoslav authorities. As Yugoslavia was at that time on unfriendly terms with Italy, it viewed the Austrian Nazis with a degree of sympathy. They remained for several months in internment camps and then were permitted to leave for Germany aboard two German ships. Altogether they were about 1,500 men.

The events had shown that the Austrian army was still a reliable force. Mussolini's active intervention therefore became unnecessary. The auxiliary troops—Heimwehr and Ostmaerkische Sturmscharen[1]—fought bravely but possessed little training. However, the same could be said of the Nazis. The course of events had clearly shown the strength and weakness of the Nazi movement in Austria. The party had a large and dedicated following in the Alpine provinces, mainly in the smaller towns and villages which were traditionally nationalistic and Pan-German. The uprising failed completely in the western regions of Tyrol and Vorarlberg, where the Catholic Church provided a strong dam against Nazi propaganda. All larger cities remained firmly in the hands of the

---

1. A Catholic paramilitary organization loyal to Schuschnigg.

government forces. Except in two towns in Styria, the industrial working class paid no attention to appeals for aid from the insurgents.

On both sides much of the fighting was carried out by green troops and not without some rather comical aspects. The rebels were partly armed with German automatic pistols smuggled in from the Reich. Many of the insurgents had never handled such weapons and did not know how to load them, so they became useless after the first rounds of ammunition were used up. On the government's side, too, a number of men were untrained and had never seen actual fighting. In Carinthia, the auxiliaries from the Heimwehr and the Ostmaerkische Sturmscharen did not know how to handle their rifles and had to be instructed by their officers while they were under fire.

The stage was now set for dealing with the captured rebels.

Holzweber was soon identified by a police officer who had served with him in the army. After the insurgents were interned, the same officer questioned some of them and came to suspect Planetta as the murderer of Dollfuss. It seems that the prisoners were given the impression that only the main culprits were to be punished. There was even talk about shooting every tenth man unless the killer gave himself up. Finally, Planetta admitted having shot Dollfuss but insisted he had fired only once without intent to kill. Perhaps he believed that the others would go free if he made a confession. In this context a brief note which he wrote shortly before his execution is revealing. It read: "Dear parents: Farewell! I go to save my comrades' lives. Otto."

The defendants were represented by three lawyers, all very sympathetic to their cause.[1] However, there had been very little time to prepare a proper defense. An effort was made to

---

1. One of them was arrested and temporarily imprisoned after the trial.

make the safe conduct an issue at the trial. Fey and Neustaedter-Stuermer were heard as witnesses. The latter did not deny
that he had promised free passage to the rebels, but he declared that their behavior toward Dollfuss had disqualified
them from being treated as soldiers. The court dismissed the
whole matter as immaterial and unrelated to the gravity of the
crime.

Holzweber and Planetta said they believed they were acting
for an already established new government. They refused to
give any information about their chiefs and about the background of the plot. As for the shooting, Planetta had already
admitted his guilt, but insisted, as before that he had fired
only once. He maintained that he had not even recognized his
victim.

The sentences were never in doubt. The defendants had
clearly been engaged in armed sedition, an offense punisha-
ble by death and on July 31 they were sentenced to be hanged.
Three hours later the verdict was carried out by chief executioner Lang and two aides in the prison courtyard. It is inter-
esting to note that Holzweber, who had refused to call a priest
for the dying Dollfuss, requested and received the sacrament
administered by a Protestant clergyman. Planetta declared
that he regretted the fatal shooting and asked forgiveness
from Dollfuss's wife. He then confessed to a Catholic priest
and made his will. Holzweber, who was to die first, walked
firmly to the gallows which had been erected in the triangular
prison yard. Shouting *"Heil Hitler!"* and proclaiming that he
was dying for Germany, he was raised aloft by the three execu-
tioners who wore black suits and gloves. They could not have
done a very efficient job of the hanging; it took him twelve
minutes to die. Planetta was executed immediately afterward,
also shouting *"Heil Hitler!"* while the noose was fastened
around his neck. The condemned men were unaware of the
fact that their Fuehrer, in his rage about their mismanaged

rebellion, had threatened to send them to a concentration camp if they ever crossed the German border. As it happened, the executioner saved them from that fate. Four years later, after the *Anschluss,* they were glorified as heroes and streets were named in their honor.

A few more death sentences followed. Also hanged was Hans Domes, leader of the second SS squad that had attacked the Ravag Building. The same fate was meted out to four policemen and one active soldier who had taken part in the Ballhausplatz raid. Hudl, who at first informed on the plot and then played the part of the false major, escaped with a life sentence. The court took his good war record into consideration. The other members of SS Standarte 89 received various prison terms.

As in Vienna, the civil war in the provinces was followed by a wave of arrests and trials. Military courts meted out a number of death sentences and a long list of severe prison terms. Of the former, only five were carried out. The logic of this speedy justice—somewhat reminiscent of Judge Jeffries and his bloody assizes—was not always clear. In Bad Ischl, two boys who had merely hidden four pounds of explosives were hanged, while many leaders of the rebellion got off with prison terms and were reprieved in 1936. Two years of unremitting hate propaganda by the Nazis had not been without effect on their adversaries, who felt that they had to fight back with any means at their disposal. Many officials, suspected of Nazi sympathies, lost their jobs. Sometimes entire families were divided, with one brother a Nazi and another serving in the army or the Heimwehr. The more moderate "nationals" condemned the revolt and the murder of Dollfuss but were inclined to play Hitler's game with more respectable methods. The heritage of the revolt was increased bitterness and resentment. A great number of persons had been injured in house-to-house fighting, and about five-hundred had lost their lives. On both sides casualities were almost evenly matched.

For the average Austrian not personally involved in the civil war, the principal reaction was one of frustration. The government had won, but there was no glory in that victory, and with the death of Dollfuss the only popular leader had disappeared. The fact that men in high positions had been willing to play ball with the Nazis added to the general feeling of uncertainty. The average civil servant was bound to ask himself: What would have happened to me, had they won? Would they have taken away my job? Fear, suspicion, and opportunism were on the increase. People joined the Fatherland Front, many just to be on the right side. Soon it had two million members, but many also gave money to the Nazis secretly or maintained membership in one of their illegal associations. The Socialists, leaderless but still numerous, kept morosely to themselves, disliking both the Nazis and the government. A popular story of those days told of four men meeting for a glass of wine in an inn. All wore the red-and-white buttonhole insignia of the Fatherland Front. When two of them left, one of the remaining pair asked his companion: "Do you think those two reds know that we're Nazis?"

15

Enter von Papen

ET US NOW SWITCH TO BAYREUTH, where Adolf Hitler was attending the Richard Wagner festival. On the evening of July 25, he went to see the performance of *Das Rheingold* at the festival house. Shortly before the curtain rose, he was informed of a report from the German embassy in Vienna that a revolt had occurred and that Chancellor Dollfuss had been wounded. According to one eyewitness, Friedelind Wagner, the composer's granddaughter, Hitler "could hardly restrain his joy." During the performance two aides continually kept him informed of the news. He was very excited but deliberately ordered dinner at a nearby restaurant where he was sure to be seen. "I must walk across the street for one hour and show myself," he remarked. "Otherwise people will believe I had something to do with the event!"

By 4 P.M. the German radio had already reported the

putsch. During the evening hours, a news story openly rejoic-
ing at the fall of Dollfuss was being prepared. But the reports
from Austria became more and more disappointing. At 10
P.M. Hitler nervously called State Secretary Bernhard von
Buelow at the Wilhelmstrasse for further word. The news he
heard was disastrous. The revolt had failed, Italy was mobiliz-
ing troops, and Ambassador Rieth had played the inter-
mediary's role between the government and the rebels. At
that time it was still thought the insurgents were on their way
to Germany under safe conduct. This last piece of news
seemed to enrage Hitler, who immediately roared that he
would either arrest them or send them back. An hour later he
declared that he would put them into a concentration camp.
In the meantime, the harassed Secretary of State hastily advised the Minister of Propaganda, Josef Goebbels, to stop his
jubilation over Rintelen's new Austrian government.

It was about 11 P.M. when von Neurath, the Foreign Minister, finally got into the act. His first move was to have President Hindenburg send a telegram of condolence to Miklas.
Another message, signed by Neurath himself, went out to the
Austrian government. He also declared that Rieth had acted
unwisely in playing the mediator.

During the next hours, Hitler, Goebbels, and von Neurath
were constantly on the telephone and the Reich's propaganda
machine literally jumped its track. With the utmost speed the
first gleeful reports turned into statements of distress and
sympathy. The putsch—a purely Austrian affair—and the
"cruel murder" of Dollfuss were severely condemned. At 1:20
A.M. the German News Agency announced that the government disapproved of Ambassador Rieth's "unauthorized intervention" and had ordered his recall. Twenty minutes later
the unfortunate diplomat received the bad news himself from
Buelow. Meanwhile the German radio furiously attacked the

agreement that called for the transportation of the insurgents to Germany. They would immediately be arrested at the border, the Germans said. By arresting the insurgents himself, Schuschnigg spared Hitler that embarrassment. It was also announced that the Fuehrer, "due to the sad events in Austria," was returning to the capital.

Why was Hitler so eager to disavow his supporters in Austria? It must be realized that, by July 1934, his regime was only a year and a half old and had very recently been shaken by his blood purge of the SA. Besides, Germany was at that time a long way from being prepared for war and any armed conflict, even with Italy, would have ended in unmitigated disaster. Hitler, in those days, was still afraid of the West. His rule was not yet consolidated. A setback in Austria, though unpleasant, could not hurt him too much. But a serious international conflict had to be avoided at all costs. Hitler was in deadly fear of "a new Sarajevo." He knew very well that Germany was still weak and could not afford a showdown. As for the Austrian Nazis, he had not the slightest compunction about sacrificing them. They would come in handy later on; martyrs to the cause were always useful. For the time being, they were the losers and Hitler made no effort to save them. He ordered the border closed, as any action of the Austrian Legion would now be highly undesirable.

At this point the question may be raised about how far Hitler was personally responsible for the putsch and, specifically, for the murder of Dollfuss. Of his moral responsibility there can be no doubt. It was Hitler who had appointed Habicht, had permitted the vicious radio speeches of *Gauleiter* Frauenfeld, had assembled the Austrian Legion on the border, and encouraged the wave of sabotage and murder in Austria. When we come to the actual preparation of the revolt, the picture is less clear. Since the beginning of the year,

Hitler himself had—at least outwardly—avoided loud threats and seemed to be inclined to let things in Austria find their own equilibrium. But by leaving all details to Habicht, he was counting on a man who was willing to risk everything for the sake of success. Habicht had been frustrated by his repeated failures and must be considered the intellectual originator of the putsch. If Hitler did not want to use violence, he should have removed Habicht from his office, but this he failed to do.

To what extent Hitler was informed about the planned revolt is open to question. We only know that Hitler received Habicht several days before the uprising. According to Goering's testimony at Nuremberg, Habicht had stated that a future move against Dollfuss by the Austrian army was intended and asked what action the party should take in such an event. Most likely Hitler approved of almost any action under such circumstances. Certainly after that conversation, Habicht felt he was now entitled to act. By that time, most details of the impending coup d'état had been worked out. We shall never know if and to what extent Hitler approved them.

On the night after the uprising, Hitler called the former Vice Chancellor Franz von Papen and asked him to become his ambassador in Vienna. Papen, who had narrowly escaped assassination during the blood purge, at first refused, but finally he came to see Hitler and accepted. According to his memoirs, he found the Fuehrer "in a state of hysteria about the folly of the Austrian party members." Papen laid down some conditions before accepting the post. He wished to see a gradual normalization of relationships through eliminating the influence of the illegal party in Austria. Though a rogue and opportunist, Papen had no use for gangster methods. An aristocrat and a gentleman, he refused to operate with bands of cutthroats and bomb throwers. He also demanded the removal of Habicht, and Hitler, only too glad to find a culprit, wholeheartedly agreed. On July 26, Habicht was dismissed in disgrace for having "misinformed, deceived and betrayed" his Fuehrer.

With the fall of Habicht and the appointment of von Papen, a new era began. The goal—complete absorption of Austria into the Reich—remained, but the methods were changed. Hitler had been deeply frightened and he was not to forget the experience. His hatred of those infuriating Austrians increased, as he amply proved by the way he treated his political adversaries four years later. For the time being, severe measures were taken against his own creatures. The Austrian wing of the party was dissolved; the Austrian Legion were transferred away from the border; members of the Nazi organization were strictly forbidden to take part in illegal groups. Discussions on Austrian policy suddenly disappeared from the radio program. Travel to Austria was allowed only by permission of the Ministry of the Interior. The German and the illegal Austrian Nazi Party had to operate now as completely separate units. None of the men who had played a major part in the putsch got any office of importance for the next four years. Even after the *Anschluss,* only a very few made real careers. The only Austrian Nazi who later rose to a position of great power was Ernst Kaltenbrunner, the infamous head of the RSHA.[1] In 1934, he was still an unknown attorney in Linz.

The failure of the uprising and the highly unfavorable reaction abroad changed Hitler's thinking in regard to the Austrian problem. He realized that further acts of violence could

---

1. Reichs Sicherheits Hauptamt (Office of Security). This agency controlled the Gestapo and was responsible for most of the German atrocities during World War II.

only worsen his situation. Therefore, he resolutely changed his tactics. Sedition and sabotage were to be replaced by diplomacy. Instead of civil war, slow, steady erosion would undermine the position of the Austrian government. Furthermore, nothing drastic would be undertaken as long as the international situation favored Austrian independence. At this point, Hitler could not possibly foresee the war in Abyssinia, the Spanish Civil War, the growing internal weakness of France, and the advent of a British government that was willing to appease him. None of these developments was clearly discernible or even probable in 1934. What Hitler foresaw correctly was the weakness of the Austrian government and its precarious position which depended on foreign events totally beyond its control. He therefore decided to wait and take the initiative only when circumstances allowed. In the meantime, Germany would arm to the teeth, biding her time. He was not too worried about losing support in Austria. Her economic situation was bad and Germany had no interest in improving it. With 400,000 unemployed in Austria, there was bound to be plenty of dissatisfaction—the best feeding ground for would-be stormtroopers.

In other words, Hitler learned his lesson in 1934, and when he occupied Austria four years later, everything worked with the precision of a well-constructed steam roller. Arms were raised only to salute the Wehrmacht; not a shot was fired; and Mussolini kept his divisions at home. It was he and the Western democracies who had failed to learn from the events of July 1934. The facts were clear to everybody and no special intelligence was required to understand them. The report, published by the Austrian government on the preliminaries and events of the uprising, was a fairly good introduction to the methods of German policy. Besides, numerous foreign journalists had witnessed the attempted coup d'état. Books and articles about it were published in England and France; the usual consternation and indignation was uttered by the press, and then the matter was conveniently forgotten.

This was most regrettable, because many Western statesmen and military experts could have learned a great deal by studying those reports. The Vienna putsch could have provided them with excellent examples of the methods the Nazis were going to use a few years later to enslave Europe. Of course, by then everything was greatly improved and modernized. But as an introduction to total war on a limited scale, the story of the July revolt was valuable material. For example, the use of stolen uniforms was put into practice on May 10, 1940, during the attack on the Netherlands, and it led to the capture of a vital bridge at Gennep. Similar methods were also used during the campaign in Scandinavia. Copenhagen was taken by a batallion from a troop transport which docked peacefully at a pier right in the heart of the city. The idea of using a broadcasting station to announce a coup d'état was used by the Norwegian archtraitor Vidkun Quisling, who named himself head of government and ordered his countrymen—though unsuccessfully—to end resistance to the German army. As late as 1944, the Germans used troops disguised in American uniforms, during the Battle of the Bulge. Several posed as M.P.s and misdirected military traffic.

Another more intricate strategy was the diligent search for willing collaborators. Had the putsch succeeded, Rintelen and not Waechter would have been the head of the new government. Now, Rintelen had never been a member of the Nazi Party; he could not even be accused of being a sympathizer, and he had served his country in several important functions. The technique of using stooges of respectable background and not too overt connection with the Reich was later developed to perfection. By 1938, two such men had been placed within the Austrian government: Edmund Glaise-Horstenau and Arthur Seyss-Inquart. Both always insisted they were not really National Socialists, that they were for Austrian independence; in fact, they turned out to be the gravediggers of their own country.[1]

The same tactics were later used in other countries, especially in France, where collaborators like Laval, Maurras, Luchaire, and de Brinon did more harm than the outright fascists did. On a lower level, Nazi collaborators in the police forces and various government agencies were in action all over Europe.

Another lesson, which could have been learned from the short Austrian civil war in 1934, was the use of small but resolute and well-trained commandos like the SS Standarte 89. During the first phase of World War II, such small groups played a very decisive role. Especially in Norway, Holland, and Belgium they proved eminently successful, as the old-fashioned military command in those countries was totally unprepared to deal with them. The city of Oslo was taken by five German companies, equipped with light weapons only, who landed unexpectedly at an undefended airport. In Holland, the most important bridges at the Moerdijk fell to a small force of parachutists before the garrison could be alerted. In Belgium, the famous Fort Eben Emael, manned by 1,200 men, was captured by eighty German soldiers, landing in gliders, with only twenty casualties. It took the Allies years to adopt these methods. Later on they were turned against the Germans with a vengeance. However, many initial disasters could have been prevented, had the military only done their homework.

---

1. Both men came to a melancholy end: Seyss-Inquart was hanged in Nuremberg as a war criminal, Glaise-Horstenau committed suicide.

As for the Austrian government, it won its second civil war within six months, but it was left in considerable disarray after Dollfuss's death. Whatever his faults, the little Chancellor had become the standard bearer of Austrian independence. His support within his country was limited, but his leadership was undisputed. He was very popular, at least with those who shared his convictions—probably not more than about a third of his countrymen.

With the death of Dollfuss the situation changed. His successor, Kurt von Schuschnigg, was intellectually superior to him, highly cultured, and a man of integrity. However, he lacked Dollfuss's rapport with the people and—except for a very brief moment at the end of his political career—never gained popularity. Under his leadership the base of the government eroded. In her far from favorable situation, Austria would have required a man of strong popular appeal with the ability to unite all available forces against the Nazis. Schuschnigg, according to one of his collaborators, would have been an excellent chairman of the Academy of Sciences. He was always somewhat aloof, without charisma, too cautious to engender much enthusiasm and too reactionary to gain wide support.

His original appointment during the emergency of the coup d'état was made permanent and official after Dollfuss had been buried with a solemn state funeral on July 29.[1] On that day, Vienna seemed to be in tears; even many former adversaries of Dollfuss were moved by his brutal death. During the next years he was proclaimed the great martyr of his cause,

---

1. Dollfuss was buried in a cemetery in Hietzing, but his remains later were transferred to a church and laid to rest in a crypt close to the tomb of Ignaz Seipel, one of his predecessors.

not only by his political successors but also by the Church.[1]

The Fatherland Front, his creation, was now leaderless. Starhemberg took over its direction. The idea was to divide Dollfuss's functions between him and Schuschnigg, but this proved to be an unsatisfactory arrangement. Starhemberg had little talent for directing a large political organization. Soon his influence began to wane and in May 1936 he was dismissed from all his functions. Schuschnigg himself took over the Front's leadership. Starhemberg left Austria shortly before the *Anschluss.* During World War II he served in the British and Free French air forces.

Fey, the second strongest man of the Heimwehr, was at first allowed to remain in the Cabinet. It was feared that his prompt removal would lead to embarrassing revelations. His attitude during the occupation of the chancellery had raised grave suspicions. There was even some talk about a court-martial for him and for his aide Major Karl Wrabel. The latter was accused of having talked very freely with the insurgents.

No definite proof exists that Fey or one of his subordinates actively collaborated with the rebels. Schuschnigg, no great friend of Fey but a fair witness, always maintained the conviction that the major was not guilty of conscious treachery. Certainly, some of his actions during the critical afternoon could be explained by the fact that Fey was under severe pressure and wished to prevent further bloodshed. Fey had been one of the most highly decorated officers of the old army, with a most distinguished record, a soldier wounded in battle six times. Such a man could hardly be accused of cow-

---

1. A beautiful memorial to Dollfuss was erected at the Church of the Dormition in Jerusalem.

ardice, but his reputation for bravery made his behavior seem even more ambiguous.

A completely satisfactory explanation for Fey's strange attitude will perhaps never be found. With all the documentary evidence uncovered after World War II, it can be taken for certain that contacts existed between Fey and the Nazis, perhaps even with Waechter personally. But the same can be said of other Austrian politicians. One of the rebels declared later that Wrabel had hinted to him that the Heimwehr had its own plan for a revolt against the Dollfuss government. Those remarks could explain Waechter's alleged negotiations with another of Fey's subordinates, Captain Kuglmayer.[1] Of course, it is possible that Fey's real intention was to trap the Nazis and that he was merely playing for time. Our conclusion must be that Fey was ambitious and unstable and probably lost his nerve on the fatal afternoon of July 25; but he cannot be charged with treason.

In any case, it was decided to keep Fey in the new Cabinet as Minister of the Interior but without any functions concerned with internal security. The government's official report about the revolt omitted Fey's strange behavior and his willingness to play ball with the Nazis. A court of honor performed an additional whitewash and acquitted him of any improper behavior. Nevertheless, Fey's political usefulness had come to an end. In October 1935, he and his friend Neustaedter-Stuermer were removed from their Cabinet posts. As a consolation price, Fey was appointed president of the Danube Steamship Company. Neustaedter-Stuermer, a strong believer in fascism, tried to establish a working agreement between Schuschnigg and the Nazis. For a brief period he again entered the Cabinet, only to be dismissed when his

---

1. See page 112 above.

efforts failed. Both men came to a dark and violent end after the occupation of Austria in 1938. Their ambiguous attitude in the affair of the promised safe conduct marked them as future victims of the Nazi terror.

Rintelen had suffered a slight stroke in consequence of his suicide attempt. In March 1935, he was tried for high treason. He brazenly denied any knowledge of the planned revolt. As all major conspirators were beyond the reach of the Austrian authorities, the evidence had to be pieced together. One of the most damaging witnesses—a truly Austrian touch—was his own valet. Rintelen was found guilty and received a life sentence. He remained in jail until February 1938, when he was released as a result of the general amnesty, forced on the Austrian government by Hitler. In his memoirs, written during World War II, he tried to justify his treasonable designs. He certainly was the most sinister figure of the first Austrian Republic.

Epilogue

THE EVENTS WHICH LED TO THE FALL OF AUSTRIA IN 1938 are not within the scope of this book. But now that the story of the 1934 revolt has been told, its consequences and the ultimate fate of the persons concerned should also be noted.

Hitler's failure to overthrow the Austrian government on July 25, 1934, could have had decisive results if the great powers had reacted to form a strong and permanent barrier against further Nazi aggression. For a short period such a common front seemed possible. In April 1935, Britain, France, and Italy declared at Stresa that Austria's independence was in their common interest. Had this verdict been cemented by a strong guarantee, the history of Europe might have taken a different turn. But only five months later Mussolini launched his conquest of Ethiopia, which brought him in conflict with the West. As Britain and France opposed his venture, the "front of Stresa" began to crumble. The war in Ethiopia was the first step in a policy of aggression that eventually ended in total disaster and the fall of Mussolini. From 1935 on, Mussolini's main preoccupation was with Africa and the Mediterranean. This and the outbreak of the Spanish Civil War in July 1936 drove him into the arms of Hitler, who now saw his chance to end the Reich's political isolation. Hitler's policy toward Austria became more aggressive when it became clear that Mussolini began to abandon his small neighbor. In the meantime, the Rhineland was remilitarized, and then a slow but very efficient policy to undermine the Schuschnigg government was set in motion.

The first step of that strategy seemed almost a success for Schuschnigg. Two years after Dollfuss's death, the so-called "July Agreement"—mainly a brain-child of the crafty von Papen—was concluded. In its text Hitler fully recognized the sovereignty of Austria and promised to abstain from any "direct or indirect intervention." Austria, on her side, declared itself to be "a German state," but the treaties with Italy and Hungary remained in force. So far, so good. But in a secret protocol, Austria promised to admit men of the "National opposition" to the government. One crypto-Nazi, Edmund Glaise-Horstenau, became Minister without portfolio; others were placed in minor posts. This was the most important part of the whole agreement. The unfortunate Austrians had to drag the Trojan horse within their own walls. Later on, a committee of seven was formed to "cooperate with the government." Four of the members were active National Socialists, who worked diligently for the overthrow of the government which had been foolish enough to appoint them. In January 1938, that nest of conspirators was finally raided by the police. The documents found indicated that a new plot was in the making.

This new plan—called Tavs plan, after its initiator Dr. Franz Tavs, one of Schuschnigg's Nazi appointees—was conceived in a very different vein from the coup d'état Waechter had organized in 1934. This time the full force of the German Wehrmacht was to come into play. The activity of the Austrian Nazi Party was the lever which would put the occupation of Austria by German troops into motion.

The steps envisaged by Dr. Tavs were:

1. Austrian National Socialists create incidents which force the government into acts of suppression. As a nice side action it was suggested that an attack be made on the German Embassy and blamed on the Fatherland Front.

2. The issuance of a German ultimatum, demanding admission of Austrian Nazis to the government and the cessation of all police or army action against them.

3a. First alternative: The Austrian government accepts the ultimatum. The illegal Nazi Party is then integrated into the Fatherland Front.

3b. Second alternative: The government cannot cope with the outbreak of unrest. Therefore invasion follows.

4. The German army occupies Austria to restore the peace.

If anyone in the Austrian government still had any illusions, this plan and many similar documents must have destroyed them for good. Schuschnigg knew that there was little hope for foreign help. He decided on further concessions. He had already appointed Dr. Arthur Seyss-Inquart state councilor. This man, a music-loving attorney and practicing Catholic, played the part of a moderate Pan-German. Schuschnigg trusted him and hoped that he would help to pacify the Nazis. Several months later, Seyss-Inquart was to claim that he had considered himself a member of the Nazi Party since 1931. However, toward the gullible, gentlemanly Schuschnigg he acted the part of the Austrian patriot with German sympathies, with a mystic predilection for an imaginary Reich, possibly a monarchy. In truth, he had probably from the very beginning decided on a treasonous course, though he seems to have been naïve enough to believe that Hitler would grant a National Socialist Austria the status of an independent satellite.

The rest of the story is well known. Schuschnigg was persuaded by von Papen to meet Hitler at the Fuehrer's mountain resort at Berchtesgaden on February 12, 1938. He had hoped to negotiate a new agreement with Hitler, but there was no question of any discussion. He was faced with an ultimatum which, in practice, came very near to the ideas of the Tavs plan. It meant the admission of the Nazi Party into the Fatherland Front, an amnesty within three days, reinstitution of dismissed civil servants and officers, nomination of a Nazi banker as economic coordinator and—most important— the appointment of Seyss-Inquart as Minister of the Interior with full control of the police forces. The tone of Hitler's threats and the presence of three generals left no doubt about the Fuehrer's intentions. Schuschnigg became convinced that rejection would mean immediate invasion and he signed although on the condition that President Miklas approved the agreement. Miklas signed three days later with serious mental reservations.

The amnesty also included the insurgents of the 1934 revolt. Many of the minor participants had already been released after the first agreement with Germany in 1936. These were the SS men who had gone to Germany and testified there about their part in the revolt. Now the remaining prisoners were freed, among them Rintelen, Steinhaeusl, and many members of the SS Standarte 89.

During the last four weeks of the Austrian republic, Schuschnigg made a desperate attempt to stop the gap that had been opened in the dike. There was a slight chance that the worst would be prevented if the loyal population and all foreign governments, who could have given some assistance were immediately alerted to Hiler's ultimatum. But it was feared that this would provoke Hitler to prompt action. Therefore it was decided to fulfill the terms of the agreement and gain time, in the hope that Hitler would be reasonable or that England, France, and Italy would take a strong stand. However, internal pressure by the local Nazis, who felt that victory was in the air, became overwhelming. They could now demonstrate openly, without fear, for the new Minister of the Interior was supporting them. The police themselves became unsure of whose side they were supposed to take. Soon it became very clear that Hitler did not respect the new agreement any more than he had the previous one. Though the Nazis already had one foot in the government, activities of the illegal party organization multiplied. In Graz, riots and demonstrations became so threatening that troops had to be sent there hurriedly.

On February 24, Schuschnigg made a fighting speech on Austrian independence with the keynote: "Thus far and no farther!" He made a belated effort to get some support from the Social Democrats, outlawed since the civil war of February 1934. It was his great moment. He walked amid a jubilant crowd without the slightest protection. But soon afterward he was faced with new German blackmail: demands for complete legalization of the Nazi party, admission of Nazi newspapers, and new economic measures. Convinced that no further com-

promising was possible, Schuschnigg decided on a desperate
measure: a plebiscite on very short notice. The fateful decision was taken in greatest secrecy on March 6, but news of it
was promptly passed on to Berlin by a disloyal secretary. Two
days later Schuschnigg announced that a plebiscite would
take place on March 13. He hoped to forestall a strong Nazi
campaign by giving his adversaries no time for preparation.
Furthermore, the question to be answered by the voters[1] was
posed in such a way that only the out-and-out Nazis would
vote No. Schuschnigg himself figured—not without justification—that he would receive about 70 per cent of the ballots.

That gamble could have succeeded if Austria had been
solidly backed by the great powers. But Hitler knew that this
was not the case, that no one would move a finger, that
Austria had been written off by Italy and by Britain. France
was once more in a cabinet crisis and incapable of action. A
flood of blackmail, threats, and forgery overthrew the government on March 11 and led to the German invasion on the
following day. The eroded system, long riddled with traitors,
simply caved in when enough pressure was applied. The
army might have resisted, had it been ordered to do so, but
Schuschnigg had no stomach for heroics. He left the political
scene with a brief, dramatic speech, ending with "God save
Austria!" He could have fled; instead he went quietly home
and allowed himself to be captured by his mortal enemies.
Almost miraculously he survived seven years in various jails
and concentration camps. One can respect his attitude. Perhaps history would have been kinder to him if he had ordered
his little army to resist and fallen, fighting to the last.

Like the putsch of July 1934, the last drama took place at

---

1. The question to be answered by the Austrian voter read: "Do you favor a free,
independent, German, Christian, authoritarian Austria?"

the Ballhausplatz. During all of that Friday, March 11, ministers debated, telephones constantly rang, ultimatums were delivered, and in the evening hours the building was once more occupied by the SS, with some members of Standarte 89 participating. President Miklas, though practically a captive, showed remarkable courage and refused to appoint Seyss-Inquart Chancellor. Finally, at about midnight—Berlin had already announced that the German troops would march—he gave in. By then some men had already climbed the balcony from the outside and hoisted the swastika. Within, complete chaos reigned; the members of both the old and new government were present and a number of Nazi leaders had casually entered the building. One of them, a certain Hubert Klausner, finally stepped before a microphone and yelled: "One nation, one Reich, one Fuehrer!" This was the end of the first Austrian republic. The legal subterfuges employed during the following days to make it disappear from the map are without great interest.

The next morning the invasion began, officially triggered by a fraudulent telegram that was actually never sent. Berlin claimed that the new Austrian government had asked for military aid "to prevent bloodshed." Even the otherwise obedient Seyss-Inquart refused to send that message. Consequently, the telegram was composed and filed by the German General Post Office. The scenes of jubilation and degradation which followed shocked those who still thought of Vienna as a city of charm and gracious living. Crowds roamed the streets howling *"Sieg Heil"* and the name of the Fuehrer, littering the pavement with leaflets and paper swastikas. The same emblem suddenly appeared in buttonholes which only the previous day had borne the red-white-red ribbon. At night the larger squares were full of brown-shirted boys waving flags and torches. A great number of persons who had only recently hailed Schuschnigg changed their allegiance with amazing speed.

As the police remained completely inactive, the mob had a marvelous time tormenting and humiliating its victims. Vienna's walls and pavements were still plastered with posters and painted signs of the Schuschnigg regime. The Nazis forced their prisoners to remove the placards with their fingernails and made them wash the paint off with acid. Another favorite sport was to make Jews or other real or imagined adversaries clean public latrines or barracks of the storm troopers. Jewish stores were defaced with yellow paint. Often the shopkeepers themselves were forced to do the painting under SA surveillance. All this provided a splendid opportunity to settle old scores and take petty revenge on hated neighbors or creditors. It must be said that the invading German troops behaved far better than the native Nazis. Austrians, to whom their country meant more than a temporary slogan, hid their faces in revulsion.

Far more frightening was the terror which started immediately after Schuschnigg resigned. Within a few days some 76,000 persons were arrested. Most of them had never committed the slightest irregularity; they were simply supposed to be anti-Nazis. All leading officials of the previous government were imprisoned, often for years. Many of them never returned.

We shall here follow the fate of only a few of the persons who had been involved in the Ballhausplatz affair. A few days after the *Anschluss*, it was briefly announced that the former Minister Emil Fey had committed suicide. What actually happened in Fey's apartment will never be known exactly. Mr. and Mrs. Fey, their son, a student at a military academy, their maid, and their dog were found dead, all riddled with bullets. The evidence is much clearer regarding Odo Neustaedter-

Stuermer. He was shot in the street, by persons unknown. We are far better informed about the fate of General Wilhelm Zehner, the third minister, who was involved in the affair of July 25, 1934. On April 10, 1938, Zehner and his wife went to cast their vote in the plebiscite arranged by Hitler to ratify the *Anschluss*. They had been advised to do so by friends who feared for their safety. Zehner, so far, had not been molested, but he had noticed that he was being watched. While at the polls, Mrs. Zehner observed one of the guards pointing at her husband. That night, two men broke into Zehner's apartment and shot him. When Mrs. Zehner and the maid entered the room, one of the men was putting a revolver in the dead man's hand. As Zehner did not even own a gun at the time, it was obviously an attempt to fake a suicide. The two men, claiming to be members of the Gestapo, then searched the house and confiscated some jewelry. Mrs. Zehner and the maid were forced to sign a declaration that the general had taken his own life. The following morning, the corpse was removed by the Gestapo and released a few days later for burial. Those attending the funeral were photographed, and Mrs. Zehner and her maid were kept under observation for a long time.

There can be little doubt that these three murders were connected and most probably were carried out by members of SS Standarte 89. Fey, Zehner, and Neustaedter-Stuermer were considered to have been instrumental in the capture of the insurgents at the chancellery. Indeed, they had negotiated with the rebels and promised them safe conduct to the border.

Possibly there was a plan to stage a trial of Schuschnigg over the same matter. The report on the July revolt that was compiled by the SS historical commission left this possibility open. However, either no grounds were found for such a trial or the whole idea was rejected by higher authority. Schuschnigg ended up in a concentration camp. His collegue, Karwinsky, was sent to a camp too, and survived.

Rintelen had already been released from imprisonment before the German invasion. If he had hoped to be promoted to some office, he must have been disappointed. He became a mere member of the Reichstag, a meaningless function, for this august body was employed merely to applaud Hitler's speeches. For the rest, the Nazis paid no attention to "King Anton." He died in 1946, a forgotten man, after having witnessed the total collapse of the Third Reich.

The men who had commanded the putsch faded quickly into obscurity. For a few hours they were actors in a great drama but they soon fell into oblivion. Today they are mere footnotes in the history books of that era. During the seven years of German occupation, a memorial plaque in honor of SS Standarte 89 ornamented the building on the Ballhausplatz.[1] Habicht remained in obscurity and was killed in action during World War II. Fridolin Glass and Gustav Otto Waechter at first got party positions of minor importance. However, they were severely criticized for having mismanaged the revolt. Glass fell in 1943 on the Eastern front. After the *Anschluss*, Waechter was appointed state commissioner for personnel affairs, but at the outbreak of the war he was transferred to Poland to rule the province of Galicia. His behavior in this occupied zone was relatively moderate. In 1944 he was transferred again, this time to Trieste, Italy. When Germany collapsed, he managed to escape to Rome and put himself under the protection of the clergy. He died in Rome in 1945.

Only two of the minor participants of the revolt gained

---

1. During 1940–1945, the German *Gauleiter* Baldur von Schirach resided in the chancellery.

some prominence in their home town during the Nazi era. Hans Blaschke, who helped Glass get his trucks,[1] became vice mayor of Vienna. It is rather amusing to note that he was later in constant conflict with the German *Gauleiter* Schirach. The Austrian Nazis were soon to learn that their German overlords treated them as a colonial people of sorts, natives whose reliability and competence was questionable.

The second man, who attained a career, was Lieutenant Colonel Adolf Sinzinger, the military traitor. He advanced to the post of lieutenant general and town commander of Vienna. His career ended abruptly in July 1944, when he became involved in the attempted putsch against Hitler. Sinzinger did not belong among the conspirators; he merely followed orders from Berlin. He had not realized that for a few hours the command of the German home army was in the hands of men who had plotted to assassinate the Fuehrer.

Happily the second Austrian republic, reborn during the last days of World War II, has outlived the turbulent past. The terrible years under Hitler and the following period under foreign occupation gave rise to a new feeling of solidarity and patriotism, which the first republic had never known.

The new generation of Austrian politicians rejected both the *Anschluss* and Dollfuss's Christian Corporate State. Many of them had been in Hitler's concentration camps. They had realized that the bitter fratricidal struggle between the right and the left had eventually benefited only the Nazis. It is doubtful whether a united Austria could have offered successful resistance to Hitler. Stronger and more democratic countries had been overrun by sheer military power. Nevertheless, Austria had fallen like a worm-eaten apple. There was cer-

---

1. See page 61.

tainly no reason to be very proud of the inglorious end in 1938.

The postwar development of Austria proved that the little republic was prefectly able to live an independent life of prosperity. This simple fact removed any further desire for *Anschluss*. That whole idea had not been born from any mystical brotherhood with the Reich, but—much more prosaic—was a consequence of economic depression. The new generation possessed the self-confidence to go it alone like so many other small European countries, which have always remained fiercely independent. As for Hitler, he had become a symbol of defeat; even those who would gladly have excused all his atrocities could not forgive his losing the war. Today in Austria the die-hards and bitter-enders are a rapidly vanishing community. Not one of them has occupied a political post of prominence during the last twenty years.

If Hitler is almost forgotten and merely a subject for historical debate, like Wallenstein, Metternich, Conrad von Hoetzendorf, and other losers, where does Dollfuss stand in the pantheon of Austrian history? The rebirth of Austrian patriotism and independence might seem to make him rise in stature. Has the "little Chancellor" become a great man in the memory of his countrymen?

That question cannot be answered in the affirmative. Few people will deny that Dollfuss was a patriot, firmly convinced of Austria's role in Europe as an independent state. He was not anti-German, but he refused to be directed by power-hungry men, who were driven mainly by greed and lust for aggrandizement. He had a sense of history and felt that Austria deserved more than the status of a German province run by a *Gauleiter*. What Dollfuss failed to see was that he could not achieve his goals without the solid support of the majority. Perhaps, had he lived, he would have tried to bind up the wounds which his guns had caused in February 1934. As it turned out, it took Austrians many years of war, oppression, and occupation to overcome that trauma.

For that reason, the new Austrian conservatives refused Dollfuss's inheritance of a Christian Corporate State. Both major parties chose democracy. The new republic had no taste for continued internal strife, private armies and rule without representation. Dollfuss had attempted to unify his nation by police methods, legal trickery and a strange blend of patriotism and clericalism. In this manner he created division when solidarity would have been most urgently needed. A quotation from Edward Gibbon with very slight alterations characterizes the situation to perfection:

Could passion have listened to reason, could private interest have yielded to public welfare, the confederate union of the republic might have healed her intestine discord and closed the Alps against the barbarians of the North.[1]

This union Dollfuss failed to cement, and therefore Austrian history will not accord him a place in the pantheon of great men. Yet in the waxworks of a troubled era he remains an arresting and tragic figure.

---

1. *The History of the Decline and Fall of the Roman Empire,* Chapter LXXI.

Bibliography

ANDICS, H. *Der Staat, den keiner wollte* (Herder & Co., Vienna, 1962).

———. *Fuenfzig Jahre unseres Lebens* (Molden, Vienna, 1968).

BENEDIKT, H. *Geschichte der Republic Oesterreich* (R. Oldenbourg, Munich, 1954).

BREHM, B. *Der boehmische Gefreite* (Styria, Graz, 1960).

BROOK-SHEPHERD, G. *Prelude to Infamy* (Ivan Obolensky, New York, 1961).

EICHSTAEDT, U. *Von Dollfuss zu Hitler* (F. Steiner, Wiesbaden, 1955).

GEHL, J. *Austria, Germany and the Anschluss* (Oxford University Press, New York, 1963).

GREGORY, J.D. *Dollfuss and His Times* (Hutchinson & Co., London, 1935).

GULLICK, C. A. *Austria from Habsburg to Hitler* (University of California, Berkeley, California, 1950).

HARTLIEB, W., VON. *Parole: Das Reich* (A. Luser, Vienna, 1939).

LANGOTH, F. *Kampf um Oesterreich* (Welsermuehl, 1951).

LORENZ, R. *Der Staat wider Willen* (Junker and Duennhaupt, Berlin, 1941).

PAPEN, F. VON. *Der Wahrheit eine Gasse* (List, Munich, 1952). (Also available in English translation: *Memoirs*, E.P. Dutton, New York, 1952.)

REICH V. ROHWIG, O. *Der Freiheitskampf der Ostmark Deutschen* (L. Stocker, Graz, 1942).

RINTELEN, A. *Erinnerungen an Oesterreichs Weg* (F. Bruckmann, Munich, 1941).

ROSS, D. *Hitler und Dollfuss* (Leibniz, Hamburg, 1966).

SCHUSCHNIGG, K. VON. *Dreimal Oesterreich* (Hegner, Vienna, 1937). (Also available in English translation: *My Austria*, Knopf, New York, 1938.)

————. *Im Kampf gegen Hitler* (Molden, Vienna, 1969).

STARHEMBERG, E. R. VON. *Between Hitler and Mussolini* (Hodder and Stoughton, London, 1941).

WINKLER, F. *Die Diktatur in Oesterreich* (O. Fuessli, Zurich, 1935).

ZERNATTO, G. *Die Wahrheit ueber Oesterreich* (Longmans, Green & Co., New York, 1939).

Bundeskammer fuer Heimatdienst: Beitraege zur Vorgeschichte und Geschichte der Julirevolution (Vienna, 1934).

Bundeskanzleramt. Das Braunbuch (Oesterreichische Staatsdruckerei, Vienna, 1933).

Historische Kommission des Reichsfuehrers SS: Die Erhebung der oesterreichischen Nationalsozialisten (herausgegeben von L. Jedlicka, Europa Verlag, Vienna, 1965).

Hauptarchiv der NSDAP. Bericht ueber die Erhebung der Nationalsozialisten am 25. Juli 1934 (von R. Weydenhammer, Bundesarchiv Koblenz).

Index